The World's Warships

The World's Warships

Fourth and completely revised edition

Raymond V. B. Blackman

C.Eng., M.I.Mar.E., M.R.I.N.A.

(Editor of **Jane's Fighting Ships** since 1949)

MACDONALD : LONDON

This edition, revised and reset, published 1969

Published by
Macdonald & Co. (Publishers), Ltd.
St. Giles House, 49/50 Poland Street, W.1
Made and Printed in Great Britain by
Waterlow & Sons, Ltd.
Dunstable and London

INTRODUCTION

THIS fourth edition of *The World's Warships* brings up to date the book first published in 1955 which by popular demand necessitated a second edition in 1960 and a third edition in 1963. The new volume, it is hoped, will satisfy the interest not only of students of naval affairs, but also those with more technical knowledge who have not to hand the much fuller standard naval reference work, *Jane's Fighting Ships*.

This book does not pretend to be an exhaustive survey of every naval vessel in the world down to small escort vessels, minesweepers, patrol boats, landing ships, auxiliaries, service craft and ancillary vessels—such a task would be beyond the compass of these pages with their full descriptive, statistical and tabulated treatment—but it does include all the modern and major warships extant of the principal maritime powers.

The arrangement of ships is not alphabetical by country, but categorical, in descending order for easy reference and comparison. All the aircraft carriers, commando carriers, guided missile ships and cruisers in the world, and modern submarines, destroyers, frigates and destroyer escorts, are fully described with technical and building data, but old and small warships of lesser countries are omitted, partly for reasons of space and because it is felt that readers prefer a comprehensive summary of the qualities of modern fighting ships to a sketchy mention of all naval vessels, however unimportant, of all countries.

Massive battle fleets with great cruiser squadrons scouting ahead and flanked by protective screens of destroyers circulating in their predetermined orbits or localised spheres of influence, now belong to the past. In the modern concept, allowing much more flexible strategy and tactics, task forces are formed to operate in any part of the world. These task forces consist of any strength and combination of the aircraft carriers, submarines, cruisers, destroyers and frigates described in this book.

In any future war fought with the newest weapons of mass destruction the rôle for navies remains clear: to search out and destroy enemy ships wherever they are, and to prevent enemies from using the seas for their own purposes; to protect the communications necessary to support war operations and to safeguard the supply lines of the engaged countries; to provide direct air support for operations ashore and afloat where it cannot readily be given by shore-based aircraft. In war two outstanding qualities of sea power are vividly evident: mobility and relative independence of land bases. In peace naval power plays a prominent part in supporting national policy overseas and in ensuring that world-wide trade continues unmolested. The latest inventions affect naval warfare by altering the character of forces needed, but do not diminish the need for navies. In emergency aircraft carriers and other warships can be brought to bear quickly and effectively in any part of the world.

Battleships are now almost extinct. They have disappeared from the Soviet, French, Italian, Argentine, Brazilian and Chilean navies. The United States Navy retains four battleships, although all except one are withdrawn from active service. Conventional cruisers are following battleships into obsolescence. In the United States Navy some cruisers are fire support ships and others converted into guided-missile ships. Only the Soviet Union built a large number of conventional cruisers after the Second World War.

But naval architects and maritime experts are increasingly aware of the revolution in naval strategy and global sea warfare caused by the deployment of guided-missile ships and nuclear-powered submarines. With their increase in size, propulsive power, range and destructive capacity, submarines are now regarded by the principal naval powers as major warships.

RAYMOND V. B. BLACKMAN.

Portsmouth, 1969.

AIRCRAFT CARRIERS

THE forerunner was the *Ark Royal*, an oil tanker purchased while under construction in 1914 and converted into a seaplane carrier. The germ of the modern aircraft carrier was in the first ship adapted as such in 1915–16, the Cunard liner *Campania* of 20,570 tons with a speed of 22 knots. The aircraft carrier proper was actually in embryo design in 1912, but it was not until 1916 that, to save time, the hull of the Italian liner *Conte Rosso*, begun in 1914, was acquired for conversion, and she was completed as the aircraft carrier *Argus* in 1918. She was the first ship fitted with a flush, full-length flight deck, furnace smoke being expelled through large horizontal ducts opening out either side aft. She had a displacement of 14,000 tons, a capacity of 20 aircraft and a speed of 20 knots. The *Furious*, designed as a battle cruiser displacing 19,100 tons to mount two 18-inch guns, was completed in 1917 with a flying-off deck forward. Later a flying-on deck was added abaft the funnel. Extensively reconstructed between the wars, a new hangar was built forward, a continuous flush flight deck provided, and mast and funnel removed, smoke being discharged from vents aft. In 1939 the starboard island superstructure was added. Finally she displaced 22,450 tons with 33 aircraft and a speed of 31 knots. The *Eagle*, begun in 1913 as the Chilean battleship *Almirante Cochrane*, was purchased on the stocks in 1917 for conversion into an aircraft carrier. First completed in 1920 with a single funnel and pole mast, she finally emerged from extensive reconstruction in 1924 with two funnels and two masts and a full-length flight deck. She was the first aircraft carrier to have the now familiar island on the starboard beam. She displaced 22,600 tons, carried 21 aircraft, and steamed at 24 knots. The first aircraft carrier specially designed and actually laid down as such was the *Hermes*, completed in 1924. With a displacement of 10,850 tons, a capacity of 15 aircraft and a speed of 25 knots, she represented an attempt to produce a floating aerodrome of moderate size. The *Glorious* and *Courageous*, completed in 1917 as battle cruisers of 18,600 tons displacement carrying four 15-inch guns, were converted into aircraft carriers during 1924–30. They had a greater capacity of 48 aircraft, a speed of 31 knots, and were well armed. Here at last were fast and capacious aircraft carriers. They eventually displaced 22,500 tons, and succeeding aircraft carriers closely conformed to their characteristics. The famous *Ark Royal*, completed in 1938, incorporated in her design all the improvements suggested by experience with her predecessors. She was the first large and fast aircraft carrier laid down as such, and she constituted such an advance on any previous aircraft carrier that she was the prototype of our existing aircraft carriers. She had a displacement of 22,000 tons, a capacity of 60 aircraft and a speed of 31 knots. Thereafter aircraft carriers, having been more or less standardised as a definite separate and highly specialised category of warships, were built in classes rather than as ships of individual design. The *Ark Royal* was succeeded by the basically similar aircraft carriers *Formidable*, *Illustrious*, *Victorious* (later rebuilt), *Indomitable*, *Implacable* and *Indefatigable* displacing 23,000 to 26,000 tons, completed in 1940–44, while the *Unicorn*, a maintenance carrier of 14,750 tons, was completed in 1943. These were followed by the aircraft carriers of the "Colossus" class of 13,190 to 13,350 tons completed in 1944–46, namely *Colossus* (later French *Arromanches*) *Glory*, *Ocean*, *Theseus*, *Triumph* (later heavy repair ship), *Venerable* (later Netherlands *Karel Doorman*), *Vengeance* (later Brazilian *Minas Gerais*) and *Warrior* (later Argentine *Independencia*), and the *Perseus* and *Pioneer* (completed as maintenance carriers of 12,265 tons). The six later aircraft carriers of the "Majestic" class displacing 15,700 to 16,000 tons, completed from 1948 onwards, were the *Hercules* (later Indian *Vikrant*), *Leviathan*, *Majestic* and *Terrible* (later Australian *Melbourne* and *Sydney*, respectively), *Magnificent* (lent to Canada) and *Powerful* (later Canadian *Bonaventure*). Details of succeeding aircraft carriers are given in the following pages, but it is interesting to note that the saga which started with the *Ark Royal* of 1914 culminated with the *Ark Royal* of 43,340 tons displacement completed in 1955. Great Britain has four aircraft carriers, while the U.S.A. has 28 (excluding those declassified as assault ships, transports and ferries). Modern fleet aircraft carriers have angled decks, a British invention.

ARK ROYAL   EAGLE

The largest aircraft carriers ever built for the Royal Navy. Originally to have been named *Irresistible* and *Audacious*, they were launched as *Ark Royal* and *Eagle*, respectively, to perpetuate the names of the famous aircraft carriers lost in 1941 and 1942. Although begun as sister ships, the interval between dates of completion produced many differences in their design. *Ark Royal* was the first vessel to have a deck-edge lift (removed in 1959) on the American pattern, steam catapults built in as opposed to fitted later, and an interim angled deck. The four 4.5-inch guns on the port side forward were removed in 1956 to allow unimpeded flying off, the four 4.5-inch guns on the starboard side forward were removed in 1959, and the four 4.5-inch guns in the two forward turrets on the after sponsons in 1964. *Eagle* was reconstructed in 1959–64 with fully angled flight deck at $8\frac{1}{2}$ degrees, new flight deck armour, 984 radar, two steam catapults, sturdy lattice mainmast, and larger island. *Ark Royal* underwent special refit and modernisation in 1967–70. Identification letters on flight deck *Ark Royal* R, *Eagle* E.

	Standard displacement	Full load displacement	Length	Beam	Draught
Ark Royal:	43,060 tons	53,786 tons	845 feet o.a.	$164\frac{1}{2}$ feet o.a.	36 feet
Eagle:	43,000 tons	50,536 tons	$811\frac{3}{4}$ feet o.a.	171 feet o.a.	36 feet

	Main guns	Anti-aircraft armament	Aircraft	Armour
Ark Royal:		6 "Seacat" missile launchers	30 + 6 helicopters	Flight deck and side
Eagle:	8–4.5 inch	6 "Seacat" missile launchers	34 + 10 helicopters	Flight deck and side

Propelling machinery	Shaft horse power	Boilers	Speed	Complement
Parsons geared turbines	152,000	8 Admiralty 3-drum	31.5 knots	1,745 (ship) to 2,750 (with air squadrons)

Name	No.	Began	Launched	Completed	Builders
ARK ROYAL	R 09	3 May 1943	3 May 1950	25 Feb. 1955	Cammell Laird & Co. Ltd., Birkenhead
EAGLE	R 05	24 Oct. 1942	19 Mar. 1946	1 Oct. 1951	Harland & Wolff Ltd., Belfast

EAGLE

CENTAUR   HERMES

These were the logical development of the "Colossus" and "Majestic" classes of light fleet aircraft carriers, being designed for a speed to operate with a task force. Propelling machinery of nearly twice the power gave them the few knots increase in speed. This class was the first to be provided with the angled deck, fitted in *Centaur* after her completion. *Hermes* was so different from her sisters as to be a new type. She incorporated five post-war developments: angled deck ($6\frac{1}{2}$ degrees off the centre-line of the ship), steam catapults, mirror deck-landing sights, 3-D radar, and deck-edge lift. *Centaur* was modernised in 1957 with steam instead of her former hydraulic catapults. She has a $5\frac{1}{2}$ degrees angled deck. Deck recognition letters: C and H respectively. Sister ships *Albion* and *Bulwark* were converted into commando ships, see later page.

	Standard displacement	Full load displacement	Length	Beam	Draught
Centaur:	22,000 tons	27,000 tons	$737\frac{3}{4}$ feet o.a.	123 feet o.a.	27 feet
Hermes:	23,000 tons	27,800 tons	$744\frac{1}{4}$ feet o.a.	160 feet o.a.	28 feet

	Anti-aircraft armament	Aircraft	Catapults	Armour	Complement
Centaur:	10–40 mm	18 + 8 helicopters	2 steam	Flight deck	1,028 (ship) to 1,390 (with air squadrons)
Hermes:	2 "Seacat" missile launchers	22 + 8 helicopters	2 steam	Flight deck	1,834 (ship) to 2,100 (with air squadrons)

Propelling machinery	Shaft horse power	Boilers	Speed
Parsons geared turbines	76,000	4 Admiralty 3-drum	28 knots

Name	No.	Began	Launched	Completed	Builders
CENTAUR	R 06	30 May 1944	22 April 1947	1 Sept. 1953	Harland & Wolff Ltd., Belfast
HERMES	R 12	21 June 1944	16 Feb. 1953	18 Nov. 1959	Vickers-Armstrongs Ltd., Barrow-in-Furness

Note. The aircraft carrier *Victorious*, 35,500 tons full load, completed in 1941 and rebuilt in 1950–58, was decommissioned on 13 March 1968 to await disposal.

HERMES

ENTERPRISE

THE first nuclear powered aircraft carrier in the world and the largest warship ever built. For a prototype ship of her size and novelty she was constructed in a remarkably short time, less than four years. The largest moving structure ever built by man, she has a flight deck with an area of 4½ acres. Her propulsion plant comprises eight pressurised water cooled nuclear reactors generating steam for a four-shaft arrangement of geared turbines. There are two reactors for each shaft, and the eight reactors feed 32 heat exchangers. She has an exceptionally broad flight deck, a block island superstructure, no funnels, a fully angled deck, four deck-edge elevators sited three on the starboard side and one on the port, and four steam catapults. She has almost unlimited steaming endurance at high speed without regard to the conserving of fuel, thus improving her offensive and defensive capabilities and reducing her replenishment requirements. She is capable of steaming for five years without refuelling. The absence of smoke stacks and boiler air intakes reduces the vulnerability of the power plant to battle damage and eliminates the possibility of radioactive or biological agents entering the ship.

Standard displacement	*Full load displacement*	*Length*	*Beam*	*Draught*
75,700 tons	83,800 tons	1,123 feet o.a.	133 feet *hull*; 257 feet *deck*	37 feet

Guided weapons	*Aircraft*	*Catapults*	*Complement*
2 basic point defence launchers for "Sparrow" missiles	70 to 100	4 of C-13 steam type	2,870 (5,000 with air wing)

Propelling machinery	*Shaft horse power*	*Nuclear reactors*	*Speed*
Geared steam turbines (Westinghouse)	300,000	8 of p.w.c. A 2 W type	35 knots

Name	*No.*	*Begun*	*Launched*	*Completed*	*Builders*
ENTERPRISE	CVAN 65	4 Feb. 1958	24 Sept. 1960	29 Dec. 1961	Newport News S.B. & D.D. Co.

Note. A second nuclear powered aircraft carrier, *Nimitz*, was laid down on 22 June 1968 at Newport News. 95,100 tons full load, 1,092 feet overall, 134 feet beam, 90 aircraft, 4 catapults, 2 pressurised water cooled nuclear reactors, 30 knots, 3 Basic Point Defence Missile System launchers with "Sparrow".

ENTERPRISE

AMERICA   JOHN F. KENNEDY

Although built several years after *Enterprise*, the first nuclear powered aircraft carrier, these two ships are conventionally powered. They were constructed at the same yard, and are grouped together for convenience as the "America" class, but they are not exactly sister ships, there being a three to four year gap between keel-laying dates during which time a slightly modified design was evolved to meet more refined operational requirements. The main differences between *America* (also *Kitty Hawk* and *Constellation*) and the first four ships of the "Forrestal" group are the different elevator arrangements with two lifts before the bridge on the starboard side and one on the after quarter on the port side, and a more streamlined island superstructure. The design embodies many of the electronic systems of the nuclear powered aircraft carrier *Enterprise*. These include an improved long range search radar system, the automatic aircraft landing system, bow mounted sonar, and the naval tactical data system. The aircraft complement includes three attack squadrons and two fighter squadrons. The four catapults are of the steam C-13 type. Boilers work at a pressure of 1,200 pounds per square inch.

Standard displacement	Full load displacement	Length	Beam	Draught
60,300 tons	78,250 tons	1,047½ feet	130 feet w.l.	37 feet
61,000 *John F. Kennedy*	83,000 *John F. Kennedy*		252 feet o.a.	

Guided weapons	Aircraft	Complement
2 twin launchers for "Terrier" missiles (*America*)	85 to 100	2,720 (4,965 including air group personnel)
2 twin launchers for "Tartar" missiles (J.F.K.)		

Propelling machinery	Shaft horse power	Boilers	Speed
Geared steam turbines (Westinghouse)	280,000	8 Foster Wheeler	35 knots

Name	No.	Begun	Launched	Completed	Builders
AMERICA	CVA 66	9 Jan. 1961	1 Feb. 1964	23 Jan. 1965	Newport News S.B. & D.D. Co.
JOHN F. KENNEDY	CVA 67	22 Oct. 1964	27 May 1967	8 Sept. 1968	Newport News S.B. & D.D. Co.

JOHN F. KENNEDY

CONSTELLATION	INDEPENDENCE	RANGER
FORRESTAL	KITTY HAWK	SARATOGA

The first six of the largest aircraft carriers in the world, able to handle any carrier-borne aircraft and to launch and retrieve aircraft simultaneously. They have four deck edge elevators, three to starboard and one to port, and three separate launching areas, with increased catapult and arresting capacity, larger elevators, higher hangar decks, deck-landing aids, more armour and improved underwater protection. The flight deck is a strength deck by reduced hangar openings, the bow enclosed up to the flight deck for seaworthiness in any weather, the island acoustically constructed to obviate external noise, and living quarters air-conditioned. Deck and funnel recognition numbers, see below.

Standard displacement	Full load displacement	Length	Beam	Draught
60,000 tons	76,000 tons	1,046 to 1,072½ feet o.a.	129½ feet w.l.	37 feet
59,650 (*Forrestal*)	75,900 (*Forrestal*)	1,039 (*Forrestal*)	252 feet o.a. (260 *Constellation*)	

Main guns	Guided missiles	Aircraft	Armour	Complement
4–5 inch	Two twin launchers for	70 to 90	5 inch	2,700 (4,742 with
(none in *C.* and *K.H.*)	Terrier (*C.* and *K.H.*)			air group)

Propelling machinery	Shaft horse power	Boilers	Speed
Geared steam turbines (Westinghouse or General Electric)	260,000	8 Babcock & Wilcox	33 to 35 knots

Name	No.	Begun	Launched	Completed	Builders
CONSTELLATION	CVA 64	14 Sept. 1957	8 Oct. 1960	19 Jan. 1962	New York Navy Yard
FORRESTAL	CVA 59	14 July 1952	11 Dec. 1954	1 Oct. 1955	Newport News S.B. Co.
INDEPENDENCE	CVA 62	1 July 1955	6 June 1958	3 Apr. 1959	New York Navy Yard
KITTY HAWK	CVA 63	27 Dec. 1956	21 May 1960	9 June 1961	New York S.B. Corp.
RANGER	CVA 61	2 Aug. 1954	29 Sept. 1956	10 Aug. 1957	Newport News S.B. Co.
SARATOGA	CVA 60	16 Dec. 1952	8 Oct. 1955	14 Apr. 1956	New York Navy Yard

KITTY HAWK

Among the largest aircraft carriers ever built, and only surpassed by the nuclear powered *Enterprise* and the eight great mobile aerodromes of the "Forrestal" group; the "Midway" class cannot be confused with other ships, their enormous funnel being their recognition feature. They were reconstructed in 1953–60 to handle larger and more modern aircraft. As converted they were fitted with the British invented angled deck, enclosed ("hurricane") bows as in British carriers, and the British steam catapult. Even before the conversion they had handled 37-ton bombers. They were the first American vessels to be designed as a class with an armoured flight deck, common in British ships since early days. *Midway* was again extensively modernised in 1966–69, and *Franklin D. Roosevelt* will undergo similar modernisation. Identification numerals on funnels and flight deck: 43, 42, 41 respectively.

Standard displacement	Full load displacement	Length	Beam	Draught
51,000 to 52,500 tons	62,674 to 64,000 tons	979 feet o.a.	121 feet w.l. 222 feet o.a.	36 feet

Dual-purpose guns	Aircraft	Armour	Complement
4–5 inch	60 to 80	3 to 4 inch	2,587 (3,854 with air group)

Propelling machinery	Shaft horse power	Boilers	Speed
Geared steam turbines (Westinghouse or General Electric)	212,000	12 Babcock & Wilcox	33 knots

Name	Begun	Launched	Completed	Converted	Builders
CORAL SEA	10 July 1944	2 Apr. 1946	1 Oct. 1947	1956–1960	Newport News S.B. Co.
FRANKLIN D. ROOSEVELT	1 Dec. 1943	29 Apr. 1945	27 Oct. 1945	1953–1956	New York Navy Yard
MIDWAY	27 Oct. 1943	20 Mar. 1945	11 Sept. 1945	1954–1957	Newport News S.B. Co

FRANKLIN D. ROOSEVELT

*ANTIETAM	HANCOCK	*LAKE CHAMPLAIN	*PHILIPPINE SEA	TICONDEROGA
*BENNINGTON	*HORNET	*LEXINGTON	*PRINCETON	*VALLEY FORGE
BON HOMME RICHARD	*INTREPID	*LEYTE	*RANDOLPH	*WASP
*BOXER	*KEARSARGE	ORISKANY	SHANGRI-LA	*YORKTOWN
*ESSEX				

Ordered in 1940 these vessels were among the first in America's massive war emergency programme. Originally of uniform design there are now a number of variants. Nineteen ships* were reclassified as A/S warfare support aircraft carriers, amphibious assault ships, or aircraft transports, with reduced complements of aircraft and personnel. In 1952–59 fifteen ships of the class were equipped with the angled deck and some with steam catapults. *Antietam* was the first aircraft carrier to be fitted with the angled deck. *Franklin* was stricken from the Navy List in 1964, *Bunker Hill* in 1966, and *Tarawa* in 1968 (aircraft transports).

Standard displacement	*Full load displacement*	*Length*	*Beam*	*Draught*
27,100 to 33,250 tons	33,000 to 42,625 tons	878 to 904 feet o.a.	93 to 106½ feet (hull) 147½ to 195 feet (extreme)	31 feet

Dual-purpose guns	*Aircraft*	*Armour*	*Complement*
4 to 12–5 inch	30 to 70	3 inch side and deck	1,300 to 1,990 (2,260 to 3,290 with air group)

Propelling machinery	*Shaft horse power*	*Boilers*	*Speed*
Geared steam turbines	150,000	8 Babcock & Wilcox	33 knots

Essex, Yorktown, Intrepid, Hornet, Ticonderoga, Randolph, Boxer and *Leyte* built by Newport News Shipbuilding Co.; *Lexington, Wasp, Hancock* and *Philippine Sea* by Bethlehem Steel Co.; *Bennington, B. H. Richard* and *Kearsarge* by New York Navy Yard; *Antietam, Princeton* and *Valley Forge* by Philadelphia Navy Yard; *Shangri-La* and *Lake Champlain* by Norfolk Navy Yard. Names in order of construction. *Oriskany* by New York Navy Yard, laid down 1 May 1944, launched 13 Oct. 1945, and completed 25 Sept. 1950.

ORISKANY

CLEMENCEAU

FOCH

Clemenceau was the first aircraft carrier designed and constructed in France from the keel up as such, and only the second warship of the category designed by the French, all previous aircraft carriers having been of foreign origin. Both ships have the angled deck incorporated, which accounts for their width, two British Mitchell-Brown steam catapults, two lifts, one of them on the starboard deck edge, and deck-landing aids. The flight deck measures 543 by $96\frac{3}{4}$ feet and is angled at eight degrees off the centre line. The original armament was to have been twenty-four 57-mm guns. in twin mountings, but this was first revised to twelve 100-mm. guns and then to eight 100-mm. (3.9 inch). The 1958 estimates provided for another aircraft carrier, the largest ever built in France, but owing to financial economies she was not laid down.

Standard displacement	Full load displacement	Length	Beam	Draught
22,000 tons	32,800 tons	$864\frac{3}{4}$ feet o.a.	$104\frac{1}{8}$ feet (hull)	28 feet
27,307 tons normal			168 feet (max.)	

Main guns	Aircraft	Catapults	Complement
8–3.9 inch	30 (capacity)	2 Mitchell-Brown steam	2,150

Propelling machinery	Shaft horse power	Boilers	Speed
Parsons geared turbines	126,000	6	31 knots

Name	No.	Begun	Launched	Completed	Builders
CLEMENCEAU	R 98	1 Nov. 1955	21 Dec. 1957	22 Nov. 1959	Brest Naval Dockyard
FOCH	R 99	1 Feb. 1957	23 July 1960	15 July 1963	Ch. de l'Atlantique (Penhoët-Loire) and Brest

FOCH

ARROMANCHES

A vessel of the ubiquitous light fleet carrier type of the Royal Navy, this ship was lent to the French Navy in August 1946 for 5 years, being purchased outright in 1951. Her engines and boilers are arranged *en echelon*, one set of turbines and two boilers being installed side by side in each of the two main propelling machinery spaces. In 1957–59 she was refitted with the angled deck at 4 degrees and mirror-sight deck-landing sponsons. Formerly H.M.S. *Colossus*, the name-ship of her class, she was a sister ship of *Glory*, *Ocean*, *Theseus* and *Triumph* in the Royal Navy, *Karel Doorman* (ex-*Venerable*) in the Netherlands Navy, *Minas Gerais* (ex-*Vengeance*) in the Brazilian Navy, and *Independencia* (ex-*Warrior*) in the Argentine Navy.

Standard displacement	Full load displacement	Length	Beam	Draught
14,000 tons	19,600 tons	694½ feet	80 feet (hull)	23½ feet
			118 feet (o.a.)	

Anti-aircraft guns	Aircraft	Complement
Formerly 43–40 mm. (now removed)	24 including helicopters	1,019 (1,219 with air crews)

Propelling machinery	Shaft horse power	Boilers	Speed
Parsons geared turbines	40,000	4 of 3-drum type	23·5 knots

Name	No.	Begun	Launched	Completed	Builders
ARROMANCHES	R 95	1 June 1942	30 Sept. 1943	16 Dec. 1944	Vickers-Armstrongs, Tyne

Note: Another French aircraft carrier was the *Dixmude* (ex-H.M.S. *Biter*, ex-*Rio-Parana*), of 8,200 tons displacement with a speed of 16 knots, built as a U.S. cargo ship, converted into an auxiliary aircraft carrier by the Sun S.B. & D.D. Co., Chester, Pa. in 1941, transferred to Great Britain as an escort carrier in 1942, and retransferred to the French Navy in 1945. She was subsequently classed as an aviation transport, later as a port depot ship, and returned to the U.S. Navy in 1965.

Of the two fast light fleet aircraft carriers (see 1960 Edition), on loan from the U.S.A., *Bois Belleau* was returned to the U.S. Navy in 1960 and *La Fayette* in 1963.

ARROMANCHES

MELBOURNE   SYDNEY

The first aircraft carriers of the Royal Australian Navy, these vessels were formerly of the British "Majestic" class, being the ex-*Majestic* and ex-*Terrible*, respectively. The *Melbourne* differs considerably from the *Sydney* and is fitted with a 6 degree angled deck, steam catapult, and mirror deck-landing sights. Both vessels, however, were originally sister ships of the *Leviathan* and *Magnificent* in the Royal Navy, the *Bonaventure* (ex-H.M.S. *Powerful*) in the Royal Canadian Navy and the *Vikrant* (ex-H.M.S. *Hercules*) in the Indian Navy. Deck recognition letters are: *Melbourne* M and *Sydney* S (formerly Y and K, respectively). *Melbourne* underwent extended refit in 1968 to enable her to operate with Tracker anti-submarine aircraft and Skyhawk fighter-bombers. *Sydney*, formerly employed in a flying training role, was converted into a fast military transport in 1962.

	Standard displacement	Full load displacement	Length	Beam	Draught
Melbourne:	16,000 tons	20,000 tons	701½ feet	80 feet (126 o.a.)	25 feet
Sydney:	14,380 tons	19,550 tons	698 feet	80 feet (112½ o.a.)	25 feet

	Anti-aircraft guns	Aircraft	Complement
Melbourne:	9–40 mm.	22 to 27	1,209 to 1,250
Sydney:	4–40 mm.	including helicopters	544 + Naval Reserve

Propelling machinery	Shaft horse power	Boilers	Speed
Parsons geared turbines	40,000	4 of 3 drum type	24½ knots

Name	No.	Begun	Launched	Completed	Builders
MELBOURNE	R 21	15 Apr. 1943	28 Feb. 1945	8 Nov. 1955	Vickers-Armstrongs Ltd., Barrow
SYDNEY	A 214 (ex-R 17)	19 Apr. 1943	30 Sept. 1944	5 Feb. 1949	H.M. Dockyard, Devonport

MELBOURNE

BONAVENTURE

The first aircraft carrier owned outright by the Royal Canadian Navy, this ship replaced *Magnificent*, on loan from the Royal Navy from 1946 to 1957. Formerly the suspended *Powerful*, of the British "Majestic" class, *Bonaventure* was redesigned and resumed in 1952, plans having been revised to provide a completely modern aircraft carrier fitted with the angled deck. Her reconstruction included the strengthening of the flight deck and elevators, improvements in deck arrester gear, and the installation of the new British steam catapult capable of launching jet aircraft. Unlike other vessels of this type in the Commonwealth navies, the *Bonaventure* does not carry a deck recognition letter, but an identification serial number painted on the flight deck. She was a sister ship of *Leviathan* and *Magnificent* in the Royal Navy, *Melbourne* (ex-*Majestic*) and *Sydney* (ex-*Terrible*) in the Royal Australian Navy, and *Vikrant* (ex-*Hercules*) in the Indian Navy.

Standard displacement	*Full load displacement*	*Length*	*Beam*	*Draught*
16,000 tons	20,000 tons	704⅝ feet	80 feet (hull)	25 feet
			128 feet (o.a.)	

Main and anti-aircraft guns	*Aircraft*	*Complement*
4–3 inch	21 (capacity) including helicopters	1,370 war

Propelling machinery	*Shaft horse power*	*Boilers*	*Speed*
Parsons geared turbines	40,000	4 of 3-drum type	24½ knots

Name	*No.*	*Begun*	*Launched*	*Completed*	*Builders*
BONAVENTURE	CVL 22	27 Nov. 1943	27 Feb. 1945	17 Jan. 1957	Harland & Wolff, Belfast

BONAVENTURE

VIKRANT

As H.M.S. *Hercules* the construction of this ship was suspended in May 1946 when she was structurally approaching completion and was about 75 per cent fitted out. The contract was cancelled and in May 1947 she was laid up at Faslane, Scotland. In January 1957 she was acquired from Great Britain for the Indian Navy, and from April 1957 to March 1961 she underwent large scale reconstruction and modernisation by Harland & Wolff Ltd., Belfast. She is equipped with the angled deck steam catapult, deck landing sights, and other British inventions, two electrically operated aircraft lifts; and she is air-conditioned and insulated for tropical service. She was a sister ship of *Leviathan* and *Magnificent* in the Royal Navy, *Melbourne* (ex-*Majestic*) and *Sydney* (ex-*Terrible*) in the Royal Australian Navy, and *Bonaventure* (ex-*Powerful*) in the Royal Canadian Navy.

Standard displacement	*Full load displacement*	*Length*	*Beam*	*Draught*
16,000 tons	19,500 tons	700 feet	80 feet (hull)	24 feet
			128 feet (o.a.)	

Anti-aircraft guns	*Aircraft*	*Complement*
15–40 mm. (4 twin, 7 single)	21 (capacity)	Accommodation designed for 1,343

Propelling machinery	*Shaft horse power*	*Boilers*	*Speed*
Parsons geared turbines	40,000	4 of 3-drum type	24½ knots

Name	*Begun*	*Launched*	*Completed*	*Builders*
VIKRANT	14 Oct. 1943	22 Sept. 1945	4 Mar. 1961	Vickers-Armstrongs Ltd., Tyne

VIKRANT

INDEPENDENCIA

This ship has had rather a chequered career. Formerly H.M.S. *Warrior*, on completion she was lent by Great Britain to the Royal Canadian Navy from 1946 to 1948, but was returned and served in the British Navy from 1948 onwards. In 1948–49 she was used as a trials ship for flexible landing deck experiments. She was modernised in 1952–53 with lattice foremast and extended bridgework, and again refitted in 1955–56 with partially angled deck and improved arrester gear. She was headquarters ship in the Christmas Island atomic experiments in 1957. She was sold to the Argentine Government in 1958, and renamed *Independencia*, becoming Argentina's first aircraft carrier. She was the only one of the original light fleet aircraft carriers of the "Colossus" class fitted with the angled deck before sale, although her sister ships *Arromanches* (ex-H.M.S. *Colossus*) in the French Navy, *Karel Doorman* (ex-H.M.S. *Venerable*) formerly in the Royal Netherlands Navy, and *Minas Gerais* (ex-H.M.S. *Vengeance*) in the Brazilian Navy were so fitted after sale.

Standard displacement	Full load displacement	Length	Beam	Draught
14,000 tons	19,540 tons	695 feet	80 feet (hull)	23½ feet
18,400 tons normal			118 feet (o.a.)	

Anti-aircraft guns	Aircraft	Complement
8–40 mm.	21 (capacity)	1,076 (peace), 1,300 (war)

Propelling machinery	Shaft horse power	Boilers	Speed
Parsons geared turbines	40,000	4 of 3-drum type	24·25 knots

Name	Begun	Launched	Completed	Builders
INDEPENDENICA	12 Dec. 1942	20 May 1944	24 Jan. 1946	Harland & Wolff Ltd., Belfast

INDEPENDENCIA

VEINTICINCO DE MAYO

Originally H.M.S. *Venerable*, this ship was another of the British light fleet aircraft carriers of the "Colossus" class sold abroad. She was purchased from Great Britain on 1 April 1948 and commissioned in the Royal Netherlands Navy on 28 May of that year, being renamed *Karel Doorman*. She underwent refit and modernisation in 1955–58, including a heavier modified angled flight deck, steam catapult, mirror-sight deck-landing system and new anti-aircraft battery, at the Wilton-Fijenoord Shipyard, at a cost of 25 million guilders. Her reconstruction and conversion seems to have been particularly successful and her unusually tall build up at the island superstructure presents a unique appearance. With a new island and bridge and a lattice tripod radar mast, and a tall raked funnel, she differs considerably from her former appearance and from her original sister ships in the British, French, Argentine and Brazilian navies. She was purchased from the Netherlands in 1968, and renamed 25 *de Mayo*, the date on which the Argentine Confederation revolted against Spain in 1810.

Standard displacement	Full load displacement	Length	Beam	Draught
15,892 tons	19,896 tons	$693\frac{1}{6}$ feet	80 feet (hull)	25 feet
			$121\frac{1}{3}$ feet (o.a.)	

Main and anti-aircraft guns	Aircraft	Complement
10–40 mm.	21 (capacity) including helicopters	1,462

Propelling machinery	Shaft horse power	Boilers	Speed
Parsons geared turbines	40,000	4 of 3-drum type	24.25 knots

Name	Begun	Launched	Completed	Builders
25 DE MAYO (ex-*Karel Doorman*)	3 Dec. 1942	30 Dec. 1943	17 Jan. 1945	Cammell Laird & Co., Birkenhead

25 DE MAYO (ex-*Karel Doorman*)

MINAS GERAIS

Brazil's first aircraft carrier. Formerly H.M.S. *Vengeance* of the British "Colossus" class of light fleet aircraft carriers, she served in the British Navy from 1945, and in 1948–49 was fitted out for an experimental cruise to the Arctic. She was lent to the Royal Australian Navy in 1953 but was returned to the Royal Navy in 1955. She was sold to the Brazilian Navy in 1956 and renamed *Minas Gerais*. She was reconstructed at Rotterdam in 1957–60, the modernisation including the installation of the British invented angled deck, new British steam catapult, British mirror-sight deck-landing system, complete armament fire control and radar equipment. She was originally a sister ship of *Arromanches* (ex-H.M.S. *Colossus*) in the French Navy, *Karel Doorman* (ex-H.M.S. *Venerable*) formerly in the Royal Netherlands Navy, and *Independencia* (ex-H.M.S. *Warrior*) in the Argentine Navy.

Standard displacement	Full load displacement	Length	Beam	Draught
15,890 tons	19,890 tons	695 feet	80 feet (hull)	23½ feet
17,500 tons normal			121 feet (o.a.)	

Anti-aircraft guns	Aircraft	Complement
10–40 mm. (2 quadruple, 2 twin)	21 (capacity) including helicopters	1,000 (1,300 with air group)

Propelling machinery	Shaft horse power	Boilers	Speed
Parsons geared turbines	40,000	4 of 3-drum type	25 knots

Name	Begun	Launched	Completed	Builders
MINAS GERAIS	16 Nov. 1942	23 Feb. 1944	15 Jan. 1945	Swan, Hunter & Wigham Richardson, Wallsend-on-Tyne

MINAS GERAIS

ALBION   **BULWARK**

Originally sister ships of the aircraft carrier *Centaur*, but converted into commando carriers in 1961–62 and 1959–60, respectively, in H.M. Dockyard, Portsmouth. A full strength commando is available, which the ships can quickly transport and land with equipment. Their helicopters are also able to disembark the commandos' vehicles. The ships have sufficient stores and fuel to support the commandos in operations ashore, and can re-embark the unit speedily. They not only reinforce the traditionally close association of the Royal Marines with the Royal Navy, but give these versatile troops greater mobility and usefulness, and enable them to be fully self-supporting. These ships are fully convertible to the anti-submarine role. They are able, at short notice, and entirely within their own resources, to adapt their helicopters for anti-submarine work. Four landing craft are carried at built-in gantries. *Albion* is similar to *Bulwark*, but embodied a number of improvements. Her extensive modifications included alterations to the angled flight deck and the removal of catapult and arrester gear, thus obviating the fixed-wing capability. In 1963 *Bulwark* was further refitted to the same standard as *Albion*.

Standard displacement	Full load displacement	Length	Beam	Draught
23,300 tons	27,300 tons	737¾ feet o.a.	90 feet w.l 123½ feet o.a.	28 feet

Anti-aircraft guns	Aircraft	Landing craft	Armour
8–40 mm. (4 twin)	16 helicopters	4 LCVP	Flight deck and waterline side belt

Propelling machinery	Shaft horse power	Boilers	Speed	Complement
Geared steam turbines	76,000	4 of 3-drum type	28 knots	1,037 plus 733 commando

Name	Begun	Launched	Completed	Converted	Builders
ALBION	23 Mar. 1944	6 May 1947	26 May 1954	1961–62	Swan, Hunter & Wigham Richardson
BULWARK	10 May 1945	22 June 1948	4 Nov. 1954	1959–60	Harland & Wolff Ltd., Belfast

BULWARK

GUADALCANAL	INCHON	NEW ORLEANS	TRIPOLI
GUAM	IWO JIMA	OKINAWA	

Iwo Jima was the first ship designed and built specifically for helicopter operations. Although officially designated amphibious assault ships, these vessels approximately correspond to commando carriers in the Royal Navy. They have two deck-edge elevators, one on the port side before the superstructure and one on the starboard side abaft the island. Designed to support and fully exploit the Marine Corps vertical envelopment concept for modern amphibious operations, each ship can transport a helicopter assault force consisting of a battalion of men with its essential combat supplies and equipment. They have modern command facilities, the latest cargo and material handling equipment, and ample space for embarked vehicles. The flight and hangar decks provide efficient helicopter operations and maintenance.

Standard displacement	Full load displacement	Length	Beam	Draught
17,000 tons	18,300 tons	592 feet	84 feet *hull*, 105 feet *deck*	26 feet

Armament	Aircraft	Complement
8–3 inch anti-aircraft guns	24 medium, 4 heavy and 4 observation helicopters	528 crew + 2,090 troops

Propelling machinery	Shaft horse power	Boilers	Speed
Geared steam turbines	23,000	2 C.E. or B.& W.	20 knots

Name	No.	Begun	Launched	Completed	Builders
GUADALCANAL	LPH 7	1 Sept. 1961	1 Aug. 1962	25 Jan. 1963	Philadelphia Naval Shipyard
GUAM	LPH 9	15 Nov. 1962	22 Aug. 1964	16 Jan. 1965	Philadelphia Naval Shipyard
INCHON	LPH 12	To be 1969	To be 1969	To be 1971	Ingalls Shipbuilding Corp.
IWO JIMA	LPH 2	13 Feb. 1959	17 Sept. 1960	30 Oct. 1961	Puget Sound Naval Shipyard
NEW ORLEANS	LPH 11	1 Mar. 1966	To be 1968	To be 1969	Philadelphia Naval Shipyard
OKINAWA	LPH 3	1 Apr. 1960	19 Aug. 1961	13 Apr. 1962	Philadelphia Naval Shipyard
TRIPOLI	LPH 10	15 June 1964	31 July 1965	6 Aug. 1966	Ingalls Shipbuilding Corp.

TRIPOLI

LENINGRAD **MOSKVA**

A unique hybrid type of helicopter carrying and guided missile armed large cruisers as regards both appearance and propensities. The design was contrived so that all the armament control and superstructure is concentrated forward, with the single combined funnel and mast almost at dead centre, thus leaving the entire half of the ship aft clear for the flight deck and aircraft hangar. Not only does the full beam of the ship contribute to the compass of the flight deck, but a considerable area extra is provided, for from the stern to the bridge the flight deck aft is flared out in a graduated continuous sponson, so that the plan of the after part of the ship is egg-shaped instead of spear-shaped as is normal in cruiser configuration. In effect the result is a fifty-fifty compromise of cruiser forward and aircraft carrier aft. Although it is estimated that there is a maximum capacity of about 30 helicopters, more like 20 is considered to be the feasible total number that can be operated at any one time in normal service, and in fact not above a handful of spot landing pad roundels are marked on the ample flight deck. There is an obvious potential ability to operate fixed-wing aircraft of the VTOL, vertical take off and landing, type. Both ships were laid down at Nikolayev in 1963, launched in 1965–66 and completed in 1967–68.

Standard displacement	Full load displacement	Length	Beam	Draught
15,000 tons	18,000 tons	650 feet	70 feet (hull)	25 feet
			100 feet (flight deck)	

Guided weapons	Guns	Anti-submarine armament	Aircraft	Speed
3 twin launchers for s-to-air	4–57 mm. A.A. (2 twin)	2 12-barrelled launchers	20 helicopters	30 knots

MOSKVA

JEANNE D'ARC

This ship is of a most interesting hybrid type. The design involved the embodiment of a multiple concept to fulfil the general purpose roles of cruiser, helicopter carrier, commando ship, guided missile ship, troop transport and cadet training ship. Not surprisingly, in such a novel prototype, she was modified several times during her planning and early construction stages. She was originally designed to mount six 3.9-inch (100 mm.) guns (now four). Her helicopter platform, which extends for nearly two-fifths the length of the ship and overhangs the beam, measures 230 by 85 feet. Her steam-raising plant is of advanced design, working at a pressure of 640 lb. per square inch and a temperature of 842 degrees Fahrenheit (450 degrees Centigrade) of superheat. In peacetime she is used for training 192 officer cadets; but in the event of war, after rapid modification, she would be employed as a helicopter carrier and commando carrier or troop transport with full commando equipment and a battalion of 700 men. Her first name *La Resolue* was only a temporary one until the decommissioning of the training cruiser *Jeane d'Arc* discarded in 1964 and relieved by *La Resolue* which then took the name *Jeanne d'Arc*.

Standard displacement	Full load displacement	Length	Beam	Draught
10,000 tons	12,360 tons	597¼ feet	78¾ feet	21⅔ feet

Guns	Aircraft	Complement
4–3.9 inch (100 mm.) anti-aircraft (single)	8 heavy helicopters in wartime (ASM machines), 4 in peacetime	906 ship's company plus 192 cadets

Propelling machinery	Shaft horse power	Boilers	Speed
Geared steam turbines	40,000	4 multitubular	26.5 knots

Name	No.	Begun	Launched	Completed	Builders
JEANNE D'ARC	R 97	7 July 1960	30 Sept. 1961	30 June 1964	Brest Dockyard

JEANNE D'ARC (ex-*La Resolue*)

ARLINGTON (ex-*SAIPAN*)   WRIGHT

These conversions of former aircraft carriers provide specialised ships, each fitted out as a mobile post afloat for top echelon commands and staff for the strategic direction of area or world-wide military operations. Facilities are provided for world-wide communications and rapid, automatic exchange, processing, storage and display of command data. In the conversion a portion of the hangar deck space was utilised for the command spaces and the extensive electronics equipment required, while the major portion of the flight deck, except that necessary for helicopters, was utilised for specially designed communications antenna arrays. *Wright* was converted under the 1962 and *Saipan* under the 1963 conversion programme. These ships have rather a chequered history. Laid down and built as aircraft carriers of the CVL type, the hull and machinery duplicated the design of the "Baltimore" class heavy cruisers. Both ships had four funnels, but the fore funnel was subsequently removed. As aircraft carriers they originally carried over 50 aircraft and the war complement was 1,821, comprising 243 officers and 1,578 men. Both ships were reclassified from aircraft carriers (CVL) to aircraft transports (AVT) in 1959. *Wright* was reclassified as command ship (CC) in 1962 and *Saipan* in 1963, but the latter was again redesignated AGMR (major communications relay ship) in 1964 and renamed *Arlington* in 1965.

Standard displacement	Full load displacement	Length	Beam	Draught
14,500 tons	19,600 tons	683⅔ feet	76¾ feet (w.l.) 109 feet (o.a.)	28 feet

Propelling machinery	Shaft horse power	Boilers	Speed	Aircraft
Geared steam turbines	120,000	4 Babcock & Wilcox	33 knots	3 helicopters

Name	No.	Begun	Launched	Completed	Builders
ARLINGTON	AGMR 1 (ex-AVT 6, ex-CVL 48)	10 July 1944	8 July 1945	14 July 1946	New York S.B. Corp.
WRIGHT	CC 2 (ex-AVT 7, ex-CVL 49)	21 Aug. 1944	1 Sept. 1945	9 Feb. 1947	New York S.B. Corp.

Note. The escort aircraft carrier *Gilbert Islands* was converted into a major communications relay ship in 1962–64 and renamed *Annapolis*.

WRIGHT (as Command Ship)

NORTHAMPTON

This vessel was originally designed as a heavy cruiser of the modified "Oregon City" class. After she was 57 per cent constructed as such she was redesigned as a Task Force (later Tactical) Command Ship, a rating unique in the world's navies, for the exclusive use of task force commanders in conducting either operations of fast moving carrier forces or an amphibious assault. Accommodation and equipment were modified accordingly, with a radar communications system of a complexity not possible to mount in even an aircraft carrier without detracting from the ship's fighting efficiency. She is one deck higher than a normal cruiser to provide for additional office space, has the tallest unsupported mast afloat (125 feet) and originally carried the largest seaborne radar aerial in the world (removed in 1963). In 1961 she was reclassified from Tactical Command Ship (CLC) to Command Ship (CC). All living and working spaces are air-conditioned. Her secondary armament of eight 3-inch anti-aircraft guns was removed in 1962, providing additional space for bunks, offices and electronic equipment.

Standard displacement	Full load displacement	Length	Beam	Draught
14,700 tons	17,200 tons	676 feet	71 feet	29 feet

Dual-purpose guns	Aircraft	Armour	Complement
2–5 inch	2 helicopters	6 inch side, 5 inch deck	1,240 (accommodation for 1,657)

Propelling machinery	Shaft horse power	Boilers	Speed
Geared steam turbines	120,000	4 Babcock & Wilcox	33 knots

Name	No.	Begun	Launched	Completed	Builders
NORTHAMPTON	CC 1	31 Aug. 1944	27 Jan. 1951	7 Mar. 1953	Bethlehem Steel Co., Quincy

NORTHAMPTON

FEARLESS   **INTREPID**

These vessels, of a new design in the Royal Navy, are officially known as assault ships, but with all their inherent qualities and their capability of operating independently might more correctly be described as amphibious cruisers. They carry landing craft which can be floated through the open stern by flooding compartments of the ship and lowering her in the water. They are able to deploy tanks, vehicles and men, have seakeeping qualities much superior to those of tank landing ships, and their speed and range is greater. They are also able to serve as command ships at sea for transit operations and as headquarters ships in the assault area. Another valuable feature is a helicopter flight deck which is also the deckhead of the covered well or dock from which the landing craft are floated out. The vessels have a new type of hull combining features of both an escort aircraft carrier and a troop transport with the basic lines of a cruiser and a dock landing ship.

Standard displacement	*Full load displacement*	*Length*	*Beam*	*Draught*
11,060 tons	12,120 tons	520 feet	80 feet	32 feet

Guided weapons	*Guns*	*Aircraft*	*Landing craft*	*Tanks*
4 quadruple launchers for "Seacat" anti-aircraft missiles	2–40 mm. anti-aircraft	5 "Wessex" helicopters	4 LCM (9) in dock 4 LCVP at davits	15 plus

Propelling machinery	*Shaft horse power*	*Boilers*	*Speed*	*Complement*
Geared steam turbines	22,000	2 Babcock & Wilcox	21 knots	556 (ship) 111 marines

Name	*No.*	*Begun*	*Launched*	*Completed*	*Builders*
FEARLESS	L 10	25 July 1962	19 Dec. 1963	25 Nov. 1965	Harland & Wolff Ltd., Belfast
INTREPID	L 11	19 Dec. 1962	25 June 1964	11 Mar. 1967	John Brown & Co., Clydebank

FEARLESS

RESOLUTION

SUBMARINES

IT was largely John P. Holland, a British emigrant to the United States, who invented the modern type of submarine towards the end of the nineteenth century—in essence a submersible torpedo boat, but it was not until the beginning of the twentieth century that the submarine became a practical proposition and took its place as an accepted and distinct category of warship. The first British submarines were of the Holland design, his rights having been acquired by the Admiralty. Five experimental boats were built to his specifications in 1901–2, of 120 tons with a length of 63½ feet, one torpedo tube in the bow (five torpedoes carried), petrol engines giving a speed of 9 knots and storage batteries and electric motors giving a submerged speed of 7 knots. The first development was "A 1", originally Holland No. 6, 180 tons, 11 knots. A 2–A 13, launched 1903–6, 204 tons, 12 knots, had two torpedo tubes. B 1–B 11 and C 1–C 38, 1906–9, displaced 280 tons with a speed of 13 knots. But in the following class, D 1–D 8, 1908–11, there was a vast improvement in design and a leap in size, power, speed and armament. External side ballast tanks were introduced, diesel engines driving twin screws adopted, a stern torpedo tube fitted and bow tubes disposed one above the other. They were safer, had greater habitability and a 12-pounder gun was mounted experimentally. Of 550 tons surface displacement and 620 tons submerged they had a surface speed of 16 knots (10 knots submerged). Considering over 60 years have elapsed since they were designed it is surprising how little submarines have changed fundamentally. In the "E" class, which continued to be built until 1916–17, broadside tubes were introduced and the hull was sub-divided by watertight transverse bulkheads. Of the Admiralty wing-tank type they displaced 662/807 tons with three to five 18-inch tubes (most mounted a 12-pounder gun, a few carried 20 mines) and a speed of 15/10 knots. The submarine war of 1914–18 was largely fought with this class. No fewer than 55 "E" boats were built. As many as 27 were lost during the war but their record was one of brilliant achievements. There was a brief reversion to the small type with the three coastal submarines of the "F" class, 353/525 tons, three tubes, $14\frac{1}{2}/8\frac{3}{4}$ knots, the first of the Admiralty double hull design; then a volte-face to the "G" class, 700/975 tons, 14/10 knots, whose armament included a 21-inch tube, introduced in submarines for the first time, as well as four 18-inch tubes (bow and beam) and a 3-inch anti-aircraft gun. These were the first genuine ocean-going boats in the Royal Navy. The "H" class were of the single-hulled Holland type. Ten were of 364/434 tons with a speed of 13/11 knots and four 18-inch tubes; 24 of modified Admiralty design were of 410/500 tons with four 21-inch tubes. Successful and popular, reputed to be the fastest divers in the Service, nine of them served in the Second World War. The "J" class, 1915–17, were large ocean-going submarines, the fastest afloat. Of 1,260/1,820 tons and armed with six 18-inch tubes and a 4-inch gun, they had a surface speed of $19\frac{1}{4}$ knots. The giant steam-driven "K" class displaced 1,880/2,650 tons with an armament of eight 18-inch tubes, a 4-inch gun and a 3-inch A.A. weapon, two Yarrow boilers and geared turbines giving them a surface speed of 24 knots. In 1916–18 they were the largest and fastest submarines in the world. $K 26$, built 1918–24, of 2,140/2,770 tons with three 4-inch guns, two smaller weapons and ten 21-inch tubes, was practically a submersible light cruiser. In the "L" class, built 1917–22, a return was made to diesels and normal sea-going dimensions, 760/1,080 tons, one 4-inch gun, four 21-inch tubes, $17\frac{1}{2}/10\frac{1}{2}$ knots. In all-round qualities they were the most successful type produced, and three served in the 1939–45 war. The three vessels of the "M" class represented an attempt to produce submarine battleships or monitors. Of 1,600/1,950 tons they originally carried a 12-inch gun as well as a 3-inch gun and four 18-inch tubes at a speed of $15\frac{1}{2}/9\frac{1}{4}$ knots. $M1$, completed in 1918, was lost in 1925 and the big guns were removed from the other two freaks. $M2$, converted to carry a seaplane and fitted with a hangar and crane, was lost in 1932. $M 3$ was transformed into a minelayer. The twelve "R" class boats completed in 1918, of 420/500 tons, were faster below water than on the surface (15 knots submerged, 10 knots surfaced). During 1914–18 no fewer than 54 British submarines were lost.

The unique giant British submarine $X1$, built 1921–4, was $363\frac{1}{2}$ feet long and 30 feet in beam with a displacement of 2,525/3,600 tons and carried four 5.3-inch guns in two revolving shields, two smaller guns and six 21-inch torpedo tubes. Diesels of 7,000 B.H.P. gave her a speed of $19\frac{1}{4}$ knots. She was the prototype underwater cruiser. When normal submarine building was resumed, submarines for the first time were given names, with the same initial letter according to class. The 19 boats of the "O", "P" and "R" classes were of a standard pattern, up to 1,475 tons on the surface and up to 2,040 tons submerged, with eight 21-inch tubes, a 4-inch gun and surface speeds up to $17\frac{1}{2}$ knots. *Thames*, *Severn* and *Clyde*, 1,850/2,710 tons, $22\frac{1}{2}$ knots were the first submarines to exceed a speed of 21 knots (except the steam "K" class). The six "Porpoise" class boats were submarine mine-layers completed 1933–39. Another descent to small dimensions was made with the "S" and "U" classes of 814/990 and 658/740 tons, respectively, with seven and four tubes and a 3-inch gun. Some 115 improved vessels of this type were completed during the Second World War. Later vessels of the "T", "A", "Porpoise", "O", "Dreadnought", "Valiant" and "R" classes are described in the following pages. 77 British submarines were lost during the Second World War. There are 45 submarines in the Royal Navy today, including 8 nuclear powered. The United States has 200 submarines, including 90 nuclear powered, displacing up to 7,250/8,250 tons. Russia has 375 submarines, including 60 nuclear powered.

Recently there have been notable advances in the technical development and operational capabilities of United States submarines, with transarctic navigation and continuous submergence records of nuclear powered submarines, and rapid progress in the construction of giant nuclear powered fleet ballistic missile submarines constituting powerful underwater cruisers. All this submarine activity in the United States Navy, taken in conjunction with the greatly expanded Russian submarine fleet, points to the certainty of intensive *sub aqua* warfare in any future hostilities. Since 1957 all new United States submarines have been nuclear powered and it is planned to have 110 of such vessels by 1974.

C

RENOWN	REPULSE	RESOLUTION	REVENGE

The first of Great Britain's deterrent submarine fleet, *Resolution*, was handed over to the Royal Navy on 2 October 1967. She was the first British nuclear powered submarine to be armed with ballistic missile tubes and the largest submarine ever completed in the United Kingdom. Her missiles, with British warheads, are capable of being delivered with extreme accuracy at a range of 2,875 miles (2,500 nautical miles) from the two rows of eight tubes abreast situated amidships. As this underwater cruiser is also armed forward with torpedo tubes for firing the latest underwater weapons she can, in addition to her deterrent propensity, carry out all the functions of normal fleet submarines. Her two crews, designated "port" and "starboard", each of 13 officers and 125 ratings, take turn and turn about on the schedule of two-monthly patrols. Her Rolls Royce nuclear reactor power plant driving a single shaft through the turbines gives her virtually unlimited endurance and a high underwater speed. Her sister ships are all due to be operational by July 1969.

Displacement	Length	Beam	Draught	Complement
7,500 tons surface	425 feet	33¼ feet	30 feet	2 crews of 141
8,400 tons submerged				

Missile tubes	Torpedo tubes	Propelling machinery	Nuclear reactors	Speed
16 A-3 "Polaris"	6–21 inch	Geared steam turbines	1 pressurised	20 knots surface
			water cooled	28 submerged

Name	Begun	Launched	Commissioned	Builders
RENOWN	25 June 1964	25 Feb. 1967	15 Nov. 1968	Cammell Laird & Co. Ltd., Birkenhead
REPULSE	12 Mar. 1965	4 Nov. 1967	28 Sept. 1968	Vickers-Armstrongs Ltd., Barrow
RESOLUTION	16 Feb. 1964	15 Sept. 1966	2 Oct. 1967	Vickers-Armstrongs Ltd., Barrow
REVENGE	19 May 1965	15 Mar. 1968		Cammell Laird & Co. Ltd., Birkenhead

RESOLUTION

CHURCHILL CONQUEROR SUPERB VALIANT WARSPITE

Larger than the prototype *Dreadnought*, the name ship of this class, *Valiant*, was the first nuclear powered fleet submarine of all British design and construction. She and her sister ships, comprising a class of five, are equipped to hunt and kill enemy submarines and surface warships, with sonar gear to detect at much greater ranges than that fitted in British conventional submarines. They have the latest air-conditioning and purification equipment, a water distilling plant, and a high standard of accommodation for their crews, each of 13 officers and 90 ratings. All the names given to British nuclear powered submarines (except *Churchill*, named in honour of the late Sir Winston Churchill, First Lord of the Admiralty during the early part of both world wars, famous wartime leader, and greatest Prime Minister) are former battleship names of the first and second world wars.

A submarine of "Improved" type (which will be the seventh nuclear powered fleet submarine) was ordered under the 1967–68 Defence Estimates, and a sister ship under the 1968–69 Estimates.

Surface displacement	Submerged displacement	Length	Beam	Draught
4,000 tons	4,500 tons	285 feet	33¼ feet	27 feet

Torpedo tubes	Propelling machinery	Nuclear reactors	Speed	Complement
6–21 inch	Geared steam turbines	1 pressurised water cooled	30 knots	103

Name	Begun	Launched	Commissioned	Builders
CHURCHILL	30 June 1967	20 Dec. 1968	*3/70*	Vickers Shipbuilding Group, Barrow
CONQUEROR	5 Dec. 1967			Cammell Laird & Co. Ltd., Birkenhead
SUPERB				Vickers Shipbuilding Group, Barrow
VALIANT	22 Jan. 1962	3 Dec. 1963	18 July 1966	Vickers Shipbuilding Group, Barrow
WARSPITE	10 Dec. 1963	25 Sept. 1965	18 Apr. 1967	Vickers Shipbuilding Group, Barrow

COURAGEOUS.   *7.2.70*   *Barrow.*

VALIANT

DREADNOUGHT

History was made when H.M.S. *Dreadnought*, Great Britain's first nuclear powered submarine, moved under nuclear power on 1 December 1962. She is the Royal Navy's first true submarine, as distinct from a submersible. Her primary role is as a submarine hunter-killer, for which purpose she is equipped with the latest developments in underwater weapons and detection. Her armament of torpedo tubes are all internal and all in the bow. Her main propelling machinery comprises a nuclear reactor of the pressurised water cooled type generating steam which through geared turbines drives a single shaft. The supply of this machinery was made under a contract between the Westinghouse Electric Corporation in the United States and Rolls-Royce Ltd. in Great Britain. She also has auxiliary machinery consisting of a diesel generator and an electric propulsion motor for alternative drive. Almost every electrical and mechanical part of the propulsion machinery is installed in duplicate to minimise inconvenience in the event of breakdown. In addition every control feature of the power plant and of the submarine is duplicated. These innovations ensure an extremely high standard of reliability which, combined with the need to refuel only at long intervals, give her the ability to undertake patrols of particularly long endurance at continuous high underwater speeds. She is fitted with an inertial navigation system and with means of measuring her depth below ice. Accommodation for her crew is of a standard which it was impossible to attain in any previous British submarine.

Surface displacement	Submerged displacement	Length	Beam	Draught
3,500 tons	4,000 tons	265¾ feet	32¼ feet	26 feet

Torpedo tubes	Propelling machinery	Nuclear reactors	Speed	Complement
6–21 inch	Geared steam turbines	1 pressurised water cooled	30 knots	88

Name	Begun	Launched	Completed	Builders
DREADNOUGHT	12 June 1959	21 Oct. 1960	17 Apr. 1963	Vickers-Armstrongs Ltd., Barrow

DREADNOUGHT

OBERON	ONSLAUGHT	ORACLE	OTUS	CACHALOT	PORPOISE
OCELOT	ONYX	ORPHEUS		FINWHALE	RORQUAL
ODIN	OPOSSUM	OSIRIS		GRAMPUS	SEALION
OLYMPUS	OPPORTUNE	OTTER		NARWHAL	WALRUS

First operational submarines of post-war design, capable of continuous submerged patrol in any part of the world. Design of hull and superstructure facilitated high underwater speed and great diving depth. Long endurance, both surfaced and submerged, whether on batteries or snorting. Propelled on the surface, or when snorting, by diesel-electric drive from Admiralty Standard Range diesels, and from a large battery driving the motors when submerged. Both air and surface warning radar can be operated at periscope depth as well as when surfaced. General habitability is of high standard, with strip lighting and air conditioning plant providing drying and either heating or cooling air for arctic or tropical service. Oxygen replenishment and carbon dioxide and hydrogen eliminators allow the boats to remain submerged without using snort for days. Apparatus to distil fresh water from sea water for drinking, and ample stowage for stores and provisions enable them to remain on patrol for months without outside support. The electrical propulsion system is of more advanced design than hitherto. All eight of the "Porpoise" class were completed in 1958–61.

The thirteen of the "Oberon" class are repeats of the "Porpoise" design, but have improved detection equipment and are capable of firing homing torpedoes. For the first time in British submarines plastic was used in superstructure construction. Before and abaft the bridge superstructure is of glass fibre laminate. The superstructure of *Orpheus*, the first of the class completed in Nov. 1960 is of light aluminium alloy. *Onyx*, the last of the class, was completed in Nov. 1967.

Surface displacement	Submerged displacement	Length	Beam	Draught	Complement
2,030 tons	2,410 tons	295¼ feet	26½ feet	18 feet	68 to 71

Forward torpedo tubes	After torpedo tubes	Propelling machinery	Surface speed	Submerged speed
6–21 inch	2–21 inch	A.S.R. diesels, electric motors	12 knots	17 knots

OTTER

FINWHALE

ACHERON	ALCIDE	AMPHION	ARTFUL
AENEAS	ALLIANCE	ANDREW	ASTUTE
ALARIC	AMBUSH	ARTEMIS	AURIGA

Originally there were plans for 46 units of this "A" class, designed for Pacific operations; but the Second World War in the Far East was over before any of the class was able to reach it, and in consequence thirty units were cancelled or scrapped before completion. *Affray* was lost with all hands in the English Channel in April 1951. These vessels offered a variety of appearances until 1955, appearing with or without guns according to operational and experimental requirements, but since then all have been rebuilt and streamlined in the same way as the American "Guppy" type with high "sail", or enclosed fin conning tower. All fitted with Snort. The modified boats now have only six 21-inch torpedo tubes, four bow and two stern, all internal, the four external tubes and the original 4-inch gun having been removed. *Aurochs*, the only one of the class not converted, was broken up in February 1967. *Alderney* and *Anchorite* were officially listed for disposal by scrapping in February 1968.

Surface displacement	Submerged displacement	Length	Beam	Draught
1,385 tons	1,620 tons	283 feet	22¼ feet	17 feet

Guns	Forward torpedo tubes	After torpedo tubes	Complement
1–4 inch (in some boats)	4–21 inch (internal)	2–21 inch (internal)	60 to 68

Propelling machinery	Shaft horse power	Surface Speed	Submerged Speed	Completed
Diesels/electric motors	4,300/1,250	19 knots	8 knots	1945–1948

Note. Two experimental submarines, *Excalibur* and *Explorer*, completed in 1956–8, were unarmed. The main propelling machinery consisted of turbines supplied with steam and carbon dioxide produced by burning diesel fuel in an atmosphere of steam and oxygen formed by the decomposition of high-test peroxide. Conventional means of propulsion was provided by diesels on the surface and main motors supplied by batteries when submerged. *Explorer* was scrapped in 1965 when *Excalibur* was also listed for disposal.

Of the four midget submarines completed in 1954–5, *Stickleback* was sold to Sweden in 1958 and renamed *Spiggen*, and *Minnow*, *Shrimp* and *Sprat* laid up.

ASTUTE

TABARD	TACITURN	TIPTOE	TRUMP

Rebuilding of the eight boats of the "conversion" type, *Tabard, Taciturn, Thermopylae, Tiptoe, Totem, Trump Truncheon* and *Turpin* in 1951–56 was drastic. The pressure hull was severed at the engine room section, the two halves moved apart and a new section built in. The extra space accommodated a second pair of electric motors, clutches between which and the original motors made diesel-electric drive possible, and a fourth battery section was added to give submerged speeds of 15 to 18 knots. All guns and external torpedo tubes were removed. Alteration of the five boats of the "modernised" type, *Talent, Tapir, Teredo, Tireless* and *Token* was less radical .They were streamlined with the formerly prominent periscope standards and aerials enclosed in a conning tower "fin" or "sail" which also contained the bridge. Of the "T" class, *Talent* (1) and *Tarn* were transferred to the Royal Netherlands Navy. *Totem* and *Turpin* were transferred to the Israeli Navy in 1965 and *Truncheon* in 1968. *Truculent* sank after collision in 1950. *Tantalus, Tantivy* and *Templar* were discarded in 1950. *Tradewind* was scrapped in 1955, *Taurus* and *Thorough* in 1960, *Telemachus* and *Trespasser* in 1961, *Thule* in 1962, *Tactician, Trenchant* and *Tudor* in 1963 and *Teredo* in 1965. *Tally Ho* (latterly harbour training), *Tapir* and *Tireless* were removed from the list in 1968 when *Talent, Thermopylae* and *Token* were approved for scrap.

Surface displacement	Submerged displacement	Length	Beam	Draught
1,505 to 1,535 tons	1,700 to 1,740 tons	$287\frac{1}{2}$ to $293\frac{1}{2}$ feet	$26\frac{1}{2}$ feet	$14\frac{3}{4}$ feet

Forward torpedo tubes	After torpedo tubes	Completed		Completed
4–21 inch (internal)	2–21 inch (internal)	65		1944–1946

Propelling machinery	Shaft horse power	Surface speed		Submerged speed
Diesels/electric motors	2,500/2,900	15.25 knots		15 to 18 knots

Note. Of the "S" class, *Sidon* sank after torpedo explosion at Portland in 1955 (salved, but sunk as seabed target in 1957), *Selene, Scythian, Seneschal, Sleuth, Sturdy* and *Subtle* were scrapped in 1957–60. *Sanguine* and *Springer* were sold to Israel in 1958. *Scorcher, Scotsman, Sea Devil, Sentinel* and *Solent* were scheduled for disposal in 1961–63. *Seascout* and *Seraph* were towed to the shipbreakers in 1965. *Sirdar*, expended in experiments by the Naval Construction Research Establishment at Rosyth, was sold for scrap in 1965.

TABARD

ALEXANDER HAMILTON	HENRY L. STIMSON	NATHAN HALE
ANDREW JACKSON	JAMES K. POLK	NATHANAEL GREENE
BENJAMIN FRANKLIN	JAMES MADISON	SAM RAYBURN
CASIMIR PULASKI	JAMES MONROE	SIMON BOLIVAR
DANIEL BOONE	JOHN ADAMS	STONEWALL JACKSON
DANIEL WEBSTER	JOHN C. CALHOUN	TECUMSEH
FRANCIS SCOTT KEY	KAMEHAMEHA	ULYSSES S. GRANT
GEORGE BANCROFT	LAFAYETTE	VON STEUBEN
GEORGE D. MARSHALL	LEWIS AND CLARK	WILL ROGERS
GEORGE W. CARVER	MARIANO G. VALLEJO	WOODROW WILSON
HENRY CLAY		

Lafayette was the prototype and name-ship of a new class of nuclear powered ballistic missile submarines running into 31 units. Launched on 8 May, 1962, *Lafayette* is as big as a cruiser and much more complex. Her sixteen missile tubes are arranged for launching in double vertical rows of eight, forming a compact group amidships along the after deck just abaft the "sail", or conning tower fin. Her main propelling machinery was designed for high speed on the surface and submerged. The operational and technical equipment on board and internal organisation are most elaborate, and as she was the largest undersea craft ever built the standard of crew accommodation was so high as to be almost incredible in a submarine where space is always at a premium. The average building time for these large and complicated vessels was little more than two years, a very creditable achievement. *Alexander Hamilton, Benjamin Franklin, Casimir Pulaski, Daniel Webster, Francis Scott Key, George Bancroft, Henry L. Stimson, James K. Polk, Lafayette, Lewis and Clark, Nathan Hale, Tecumseh, Ulysses S. Grant* and *Will Rogers* were built by the Electric Boat Division; *George D. Marshall, George Washington Carver, Henry Clay, James Madison, James Monroe, John Calhoun, Sam Rayburn, Simon Bolivar* and *Von Steuben* by the Newport News Shipbuilding and Dry Dock Company; *Andrew Jackson, Daniel Boone, Kamehameha, Mariano G. Vallejo, Stonewall Jackson* and *Woodrow Wilson* by Mare Island Naval Shipyard; and *John Adams* and *Nathanael Greene* by Portsmouth Naval Shipyard. *Lafayette* was commissioned on 23 April, 1963, and the last of the class, *Will Rogers*, on 1 April 1967.

Surface displacement	Submerged displacement	Length	Beam	Draught	Complement
7,250 tons	8,250 tons	425 feet	33 feet	31½ feet	140

Missile tubes	Torpedo tubes	Propelling machinery	Nuclear reactors	Surface speed	Submerged speed
16 "Polaris" or "Poseidon" fleet ballistic	4-21 inch	Geared steam turbines Diesel generators Electric motors	1 pressurised water cooled	20 knots	30 knots

WILL ROGERS

ETHAN ALLEN   **THOMAS A. EDISON**   **ABRAHAM LINCOLN**   **ROBERT E. LEE**
JOHN MARSHALL **THOMAS JEFFERSON**   **GEORGE WASHINGTON**   **THEODORE ROOSEVELT**
SAM HOUSTON   **PATRICK HENRY**

Ethan Allen was the lead ship in a second class of five nuclear powered ballistic missile submarines, larger than the first five of the "George Washington" class. Of improved type over the first group, one big difference being that the hull was specially designed to accommodate the missiles, whereas the hulls of the first five were adapted from previous hull designs. Their "Polaris" missiles were of the "A-2" model with a range of 1,725 miles, now replaced by the "A-3" model with a range of 2,875 miles, compared with the 1,380 miles of the "A-1" model originally in the "George Washington" class.

  George Washington was the world prototype of ballistic missile armed nuclear powered submarines, and with her was initiated a new system of nomenclature, for she and her sisters, consistent with their status as deterrent vehicles, were named after presidents, generals and other prominent men in United States history, a departure from the traditional American procedure of naming all submarines after fishes or marine creatures. They have whale-shaped hulls. In addition to the steam-raising reactor and geared turbines each ship has an auxiliary diesel engine and electric batteries, both of which can be used for emergency propulsion.

  Ethan Allen, George Washington, Patrick Henry and *Thomas A. Edison* were built by the Electric Boat Division of the General Dynamics Corporation, Groton, Connecticut; *John Marshall, Robert E. Lee, Sam Houston* and *Thomas Jefferson* by the Newport News Shipbuilding and Dry Dock Company, Newport News, Virginia; *Theodore Roosevelt* by Mare Island Naval Shipyard, California; and *Abraham Lincoln* by Portsmouth Naval Shipyard, New Hampshire. All were laid down between 1 Nov. 1957 and 3 Feb. 1961 and completed between 15 Nov. 1959 and 4 Jan. 1963, the average building time being about two years.

Surface displacement	Submerged displacement	Length	Beam	Draught	Complement
6,900 tons (*Ethan Allen* class)	7,900 tons	410½ feet	33 feet	30 feet	112
6,010 tons (*George Washington* class)	6,700 tons	381⅔ feet	33 feet	29 feet	112

Missile tubes	Torpedo tubes	Propelling machinery	Nuclear reactors	Surface speed	Speed submerged
16 "A-3" model "Polaris" fleet ballistic	4–21 inch	Geared steam turbines Diesel generators Electric motors	1 pressurised water cooled	20 knots	30 knots

ETHAN ALLEN

ASPRO	**FLYING FISH**	**HADDO**	**PARGO**	**QUEENFISH**	**STURGEON**
BARB	**GUITARRO**	**HADDOCK**	**PERMIT**	**RAY**	**SUNFISH**
BERGALL	**GURNARD**	**HAMMERHEAD**	**PINTADO**	**SANDLANCE**	**TAUTOG**
BLUEFISH	**GATO**	**HAWKBILL**	**PLUNGER**	**SEADEVIL**	**TINOSA**
DACE	**GRAYLING**	**JACK**	**POGY**	**SEAHORSE**	**TREPANG**
FINBACK	**GREENLING**	**LAPON**	**POLLACK**	**SPADEFISH**	**WHALE**
FLASHER	**GUARDFISH**	**NARWHAL**	**PUFFER**		

Nuclear powered attack submarines of improved design with "tear-drop" hull configuration, and diving planes attached to the "sail" or conning tower fin, instead of the bow, to improve manoeuvrability. Torpedo tubes in both sides of the hull amidships instead of in the bow. Capable of diving deeper and running more quietly at high speeds than earlier United States submarines. Diving and steering operations controlled automatically through push buttons. Anti-submarine weapons comprise SUBROC (submarine rocket) combination torpedo and ballistic missile fired from a conventional 21 inch torpedo tube after which it streaks for the surface, leaves the water in a ballistic trajectory, re-enters several miles from the launching submarine and becomes a submarine-hunting torpedo. Either a high explosive or nuclear warhead can be fitted. This rocket was designed to give the submarines a potent weapon to make maximum use of their long-range sonar. *Bergall, Bluefish, Flasher, Flying Fish, Greenling, Gato, Narwhal, Pargo, Seahorse, Sturgeon* and *Trepang* were built by the Electric Boat Division of the General Dynamics Corporation, Groton, Connecticut; *Aspro, Barb, Dace, Haddock, Pogy, Puffer,* and *Tautog* by Ingalls Shipbuilding Corporation, Pascagoula, Mississippi; *Guitarro, Gurnard, Hawkbill, Permit, Pintado* and *Plunger* by Mare Island Naval Shipyard, California; *Finback, Hammerhead, Lapon, Queenfish, Ray, Sea Devil* and *Spadefish* by Newport News Shipbuilding & Dry Dock Company *Pollack. Haddock* and *Guardfish* by the New York Shipbuilding Corporation, Camden, New Jersey; *Grayling, Jack, Sandlance, Thresher* and *Tinosa* by Portsmouth Naval Shipyard, New Hampshire; and *Sunfish* and *Whale* by the Bethlehem Steel Company, Quincy, Massachusetts. The first and name-ship of the class, *Thresher*, laid down on 28 May, 1958, launched on 9 July, 1960, and commissioned on 3 August ,1961, was lost on 10 April, 1963. The earlier 13 boats are known as the "Permit" (ex-"Thresher") class, and 26 later boats as the "Sturgeon" class. *Narwhal* is of different design, being the largest nuclear powered fleet submarine with an improved propulsion system.

Surface displacement	Submerged displacement	Length	Beam	Draught	Complement
3,750 to 4,450 tons	4,300 to 5,350 tons	278½ to 303 feet	31⅔ to 38 feet	25¼ to 29 feet	94 to 107

Anti-submarine weapons	Torpedo tubes	Propelling machinery	Nuclear reactors	Surface speed	Submerged speed
SUBROC (submarine rocket) combination torpedo and ballistic missile	4–21 inch	Geared steam turbines Diesel generators Electric motors	1 pressurised water cooled	20 knots	30 + knots

STURGEON

PERMIT

HALIBUT	TULLIBEE	TRITON

Halibut was the United States Navy's only guided missile nuclear-powered submarine, and the first submarine ever designed and constructed specifically to launch guided missiles. Hull designed primarily to provide stable launching platform rather than for speed or manoeuvrability. Built by Mare Island Naval Shipyard. Laid down on 11 April 1957, launched on 9 January 1959 and commissioned on 4 January 1960. Reclassified as attack submarine in 1965 and missile equipment removed.

Tullibee was the first nuclear-powered submarine designed for anti-submarine warfare Equipped with unique sound-proofing. The placing of the torpedo tubes amidships allowed for an unprecedented number of sonar tracking transducers and hydrophones in the bow area which provide "ears" for detecting enemy submarines. Built by General Dynamics (Electric Boat). Laid down on 26 May 1958, launched on 27 April 1960 and commissioned on 9 November 1960.

Triton was the United States' first nuclear-powered radar picket submarine, the longest submarine ever built, and the first to be powered with two reactors. She was designed to serve as an early warning station and to keep up with the fastest aircraft carriers and destroyers. Built by General Dynamics (Electric Boat). Laid down on 21 May 1956, launched on 19 August 1958 and commissioned on 10 November 1959. Reclassified from SSRN (radar picket) to SSN (attack) status in March 1961.

	Surface displacement	Submerged displacement	Length	Beam	Draught	Complement
Halibut:	3,850 tons	5,000 tons	350 feet	29 feet	$21\frac{1}{2}$ feet	97
Tullibee:	2,317 tons	2,640 tons	$272\frac{3}{4}$ feet	24 feet	21 feet	56
Triton:	5,940 tons	7,780 tons	$447\frac{1}{2}$ feet	37 feet	24 feet	148

	Torpedo tubes	Propelling machinery	Nuclear reactors	Surface speed	Submerged speed
Halibut:	4–21 inch	Geared steam turbines	1 water cooled	15 knots	20 knots
Tullibee:	4–21 inch	Geared steam turbines	1 water cooled	15 knots	20 knots
Triton:	6–21 inch	Geared steam turbines	2 water cooled	27 knots	30 knots

TRITON

SCAMP	SHARK	SNOOK	SARGO	SKATE	SEAWOLF
SCULPIN	SKIPJACK		SEADRAGON	SWORDFISH	NAUTILUS

Characteristics of the prototype *Skipjack* are shark-shaped hull, single screw propulsion, and hydro-wings or diving planes on the conning tower "fin" or "sail", as it is called in nuclear-powered submarines, instead of bow hydroplanes. *Scamp*, *Sculpin*, *Shark*, *Skipjack* and *Snook* had improved "tear-drop" hull design and configuration. *Scorpion* of this class was lost in the Atlantic in May 1968.

Sargo, *Seadragon* and *Swordfish* are sister ships of *Skate*, the first nuclear-powered submarine designed for quantity production, which completed the second submerged crossing of the North Pole on 8 August 1958 after having held the (then) record of 31 days submerged.

Seawolf is a developmental nuclear-powered submarine which broke the record when she remained submerged for sixty days in the Atlantic from 6 August to 6 October 1958.

Nautilus, the world's first nuclear-powered vessel, made history when she got under way on 17 January 1955, and again when she made the first submerged crossing of the North Pole on 3 August 1958. She travelled 62,559 miles on the original core of enriched uranium.

	Surface displacement	Submerged displacement	Length	Beam	Draught	Complement
'Skipjack" class:	3,075 tons	3,500 tons	252 feet	32 feet	28 feet	93
"Skate" class:	2,570 tons	2,861 tons	268 feet	25 feet	21 feet	95
Seawolf:	3,721 tons	4,287 tons	338 feet	28 feet	22 feet	105
Nautilus:	3,532 tons	4,040 tons	320 feet	28 feet	22 feet	105

	Torpedo tubes	Propelling machinery	Nuclear reactors	Speed	Completed
"Skipjack" class:	6–21 inch	Geared steam turbines	1 water cooled	20/30 knots	1959–1961
"Skate" class:	6–21 inch	Geared steam turbines	1 water cooled	20/35 knots	1957–1959
Seawolf:	6–21 inch	Geared steam turbines	1 water cooled	19/22 knots	1957
Nautilus:	6–21 inch	Geared steam turbines	1 water cooled	20/23 knots	1954

SARGO

NAUTILUS

BARBEL	GRAYBACK	DARTER	SAILFISH	ALBACORE	DOLPHIN
BLUEBACK	GROWLER		SALMON		
BONEFISH					

Barbel, *Blueback* and *Bonefish* were the last conventionally powered combatant submarines to be built by the United States, but while they have orthodox diesel propulsion they have "Albacore" type hull configuration and greater underwater attack capabilities. Completed in 1959–60.

Grayback and *Growler*, originally designed as attack submarines and conventionally engined with diesels, were completed in 1958 as guided-missile submarines to handle "Regulus" weapons from twin-cylinder-shaped hangars faired into the upper forward hull. Reclassified as transport submarines in 1968.

Darter, a high speed attack submarine designed for significantly higher underwater speed, and completed in 1956, is operated from a central console adjacent to the sound-proof diesel engine-room, and is officially described as an exceptionally quiet submarine.

Sailfish and *Salmon* were radar picket submarines completed in 1956 and fitted with an air control centre. Reclassified as attack submarines in 1961. *Salmon* reclassified AGSS in 1968 for DSRV evaluation.

Albacore is a high-speed experimental submarine and hydrodynamic test vehicle, completed in 1953. Conventionally powered, but of radical design with new hull form making her faster and more manoeuvrable than any other conventional submarine. Streamlined and whale-shaped without flat-topped deck, the conning tower being modelled on fish's dorsal fin.

Dolphin is an auxiliary submarine specifically designed for deep diving operations. Built in 1962–68.

Class	Displacement	Length	Beam	Draught	Propelling machinery	Speed
"BARBEL"	2,150/2,895 tons	219 feet	29 feet	19 feet	Diesels/Electric motors	15/25 knots
"GRAYBACK"	2,287/3,638 tons	322 feet	30 feet	19 feet	Diesels/Electric motors	20/17 knots
"DARTER"	1,720/2,388 tons	269 feet	27 feet	19 feet	Diesels/Electric motors	17/25 knots
"SAILFISH"	2,625/3,168 tons	350 feet	29 feet	18 feet	Diesels/Electric motors	20/15 knots
"ALBACORE"	1,517/1,847 tons	204 feet	27 feet	18 feet	Diesels/Electric motors	25/33 knots
"DOLPHIN"	750/930 tons	152 feet	19 feet	16 feet	Diesels/Electric motors	12/12 knots

GROWLER

BLUEBACK

GUDGEON	AMBERJACK	IREX	QUILLBACK	SIRAGO	TORSK
HARDER	ARGONAUT	MEDREGAL	REMORA	SPINAX	TRUMPETFISH
TANG	CUTLASS	ODAX	REQUIN	TENCH	TRUTTA
TRIGGER	GRAMPUS	PICKEREL	RUNNER	THORNBACK	TUSK
TROUT	GRENADIER	POMODON	SEA LEOPARD	TIGRONE	VOLADOR
WAHOO				TIRANTE	

The first six named were post-war high-speed attack submarines, the latter were of war-time construction. A number of the earlier units were converted, with extra batteries, into "Guppy" type. This name is an Americanism from the initials GUPP (Greater Underwater Propulsive Power), and implies a streamlined submarine, with external fittings faired into the hull or conning tower. The "Tench" class were completed between July 1944 and September 1946. The "Tang" class were completed from October 1951 to November 1952. Of the "Tench" class, *Requin*, *Tigrone* and *Spinax* were converted into radar picket submarines; *Unicorn* and *Walrus*, construction of which was suspended after the Second World War, were scrapped in 1959; *Toro* was sunk off Cape Cod on 15 May 1963 as a sonar target in an attempt to find the lost *Thresher*; *Conger*, *Corsair* and *Sarda* were stricken from the list in 1963; and *Diablo* was transferred to Pakistan in 1964.

	Surface displacement	Submerged displacement	Length	Beam	Draught	Torpedo tubes
("Tang" class)	2,100 tons	2,400 tons	269 or 278 feet	$27\frac{1}{3}$ feet	19 feet	8–21 inch
("Tench" class)	1,840 tons	2,400 tons	$307\frac{1}{2}$ to $326\frac{1}{2}$ feet	$27\frac{1}{4}$ feet	17 feet	10–21 inch

	Propelling machinery	Shaft horse power	Surface speed	Submerged speed	Complement
("Tang")	Diesel/electric motors	4,500/5,600	15 or 20 knots	18 knots	83
("Tench")	Diesel/electric motors	4,800 to 6,400/4,610 to 5,400	20 knots	15 knots	85

Note. There are also the training submarines *Barracuda* of 765/1,160 tons, completed in 1951 (*Bass* and *Bonita* were stricken in 1965); *Mackerel* and *Marlin* of 303/347 tons, completed in 1953; and the midget submarine X1 of 31/36 tons, completed in 1955.

TRIGGER

GRENADIER

ARCHERFISH	BUGARA	CLAMAGORE	HALFBEAK	PIPER	SEA LION
ATULE	CABEZON	COBBLER	HARDHEAD	POMFRET	SEA OWL
BANG	CABRILLA	CORPORAL	JALLAO	RAZORBACK	SEA POACHER
BATFISH	CAIMAN	CREVALLE	LING	RONCADOR	SEA ROBIN
BAYA	CARBONERO	CUBERA	LIONFISH	RONQUIL	SEGUNDO
BECUNA	CARP	CUSK	MENHADEN	SABALO	SENNET
BILLFISH	CATFISH	DIODON	PAMPANITO	SABLEFISH	STERLET
BLACKFIN	CHARR	DOGFISH	PARCHE	SEACAT	THREADFIN
BLENNY	CHIVO	ENTREMEDOR	PERCH	SEADOG	TIRU
BOWFIN	CHOPPER	GREENFISH	PICADA	SEAFOX	

The particulars given below are for the standard design of the "Balao" class, but 31 units were converted into "Guppies", *Barbero* into a guided-missile submarine, *Baya* and *Manta* into experimental submarines, *Burrfish* into a radar picket submarine, *Guavina* into a submarine oiler, and *Perch* and *Sealion* into transport submarines. *Apogon* was sunk in 1946, *Skate* in 1948, and *Cochino* in 1949, *Stickleback* was rammed and sank in 1958. *Lancetfish*, suspended after the Second World War, was scrapped in 1959. *Dragonet* was stricken in 1961 and expended as a target. *Aspro, Balao, Barbero, Dentuda, Devilfish, Guavina, Hackleback, Loggerhead, Manta, Moray, Pintado, Pipefish, Piranha, Queenfish, Redfish, Sea Devil, Seahorse, Spadefish, Spikefish* and *Trepang* were stricken from the list in 1962–67.

Surface displacement	Submerged displacement	Length	Beam	Draught
1,816 tons	2,425 tons	306 to 311½ feet	27 feet	17 feet

Main guns	Anti-aircraft guns	Forward torpedo tubes	After torpedo tubes	Complement
1 or 2–5 inch (removed)	2–40 mm. (removed)	6–21 inch	4–21 inch	74 to 85

Propelling machinery	Shaft horse power	Surface speed	Submerged speed
Diesels/electric motors	4,800 to 6,500/4,610 to 5,400	18 to 20 knots	10 knots ("Guppies" 15 to 17.25 knots)

The following were transferred: *Bergall, Blower, Blueback, Boarfish, Brill, Bumper, Chub, Guitarro, Hammerhead, Mapiro, Mero,* to Turkey in 1948–60, *Kraken* to Spain in 1959, *Hawkbill* and *Icefish* to *Netherlands* in 1953, *Lizardfish* to Italy in 1960, *Tilefish* to Venezuela in 1960, *Lamprey* and *Macabi* to Argentina in 1960, *Springer* to Chile in 1961, *Burrfish* to Canada in 1961, *Spot* to Chile in 1962, *Plaice* and *Sandlance* to Brazil in 1963, *Scabbardfish* to Greece in 1965, *Besugo* and *Capitaine* to Italy in 1966.
Of the similar but earlier units of the "Gato" class the following survive as research, training or auxiliary submarines: *Angler, Bashaw, Bluegill, Bream, Cavalla, Cobia, Cod, Croaker, Grouper, Rasher, Raton, Redfin, Rock, Silversides* and *Tunny.*

CLAMAGORE

GREENFISH

20 "E 2" CLASS   5 "E 1" CLASS   5 "H 2" CLASS   15 "H 1" CLASS   15 "N" CLASS

The "E 2" class constitutes a sub-group the design of which is evidently a development of that of the "E 1" sub-group lengthened to accommodate two more missile launchers.

The "E 1" class are nuclear powered fast ocean going submarines of streamlined design, fitted with six missiles in tubes which elevate out of the flush deck, with launchers two abreast.

The "H 2" class are similar to the "H 1" class but have ballistic missile equipment like that in the missile armed but conventionally powered submarines of the "G" class.

The "H" class are nuclear powered fast long range submarines armed with ballistic missiles of upwards of 380 nautical miles range.

The "N" class are nuclear powered attack submarines designed as anti-submarine hunter-killers, but are otherwise basically similar, in main particulars, to the "H" class.

Surface displacement	Submerged displacement	Length	Beam	Draught	Complement
"E 2" class, 5,600 tons	5,600 tons	394 feet	33 feet	27 feet	100
"E 1" class, 4,600 tons	5,000 tons	385 feet	33 feet	27 feet	92
"H 2" class. 3,700 tons	4,100 tons	344 feet	33 feet	25 feet	90
"H 1" class, 3,500 tons	4,000 tons	344 feet	33 feet	25 feet	90
"N" class, 3,500 tons	4,000 tons	360 feet	32 feet	24 feet	88

Missile tubes	Torpedo tubes	Propelling machinery	Speed
"E 2" class, 8 "Shaddock"	6–21 inch	Geared steam turbines, nuclear reactors	22–25 knots
"E 1" class, 6 "Shaddock"	6–21 inch	Geared steam turbines, nuclear reactors	20–25 knots
"H 2" class, 5 "Sark"	6–21 inch	Geated steam turbines, nuclear reactors	25–25 knots
"H 1" class, 3 "Serb"	6–21 inch	Geared steam turbines, nuclear reactors	25–30 knots
"N" class	6–21 inch	Geared steam turbines, nuclear reactors	25–30 knots

"N" Class

"F" Class

"ZV" Class

The "F" class are large attack submarines of an improved "Z" type with greater depth. They are equipped with snort breathing trunk for their conventional engines.

The "G" class are large ballistic missile firing submarines with an extensive conning tower fitted with three vertically mounted tubes and hatches for launching missiles with a range of 350 miles. They are conventionally powered.

The "J" class were a new type of medium submarines with a long superstructure fin and high surface freeboard. The prototype launched in 1962 left the Baltic in 1963 and several followed in succession. They appear to have been experimental vessels in preparation for the "E" class.

The "R" class in design were of a modified "W" type intended for anti-submarine warfare, with modernised superstructure, conning tower fin and sonar installation. Some thirteen boats were launched in 1959 to 1962.

	Surface displacement	Submerged displacement	Length	Beam	Draught	Complement
"F" class:	2,000 tons	2,300 tons	300 feet	27 feet	19 feet	70
"G" class:	2,350 tons	2,800 tons	320 feet	28 feet	22 feet	86
"J" class:	1,800 tons	2,500 tons	328 feet	27 feet	20 feet	75
"R" class:	1,100 tons	1,600 tons	246 feet	24 feet	$14\frac{1}{2}$ feet	65

	Missile tubes	Torpedo tubes	Propelling machinery	Surface speed	Submerged speed
"F" class:		8–21 inch	Diesels, electric motors	20 knots	15 knots
"G" class:	3 "Sark"	6–21 inch	Diesels, electric motors	$17\frac{1}{2}$ knots	17 knots
"J" class"	4 "Shaddock"	6–21 inch	Diesels, electric motors	19 knots	15 knots
"R" class:		6–21 inch	Diesels, electric motors	$18\frac{1}{2}$ knots	15 knots

"G" Class

10 "ZV" CLASS   20 "Z" CLASS   170 "W" CLASS   25 "Q" CLASS

The "ZV" class are basically of "Z" class design but converted to ballistic missile submarines with larger conning towers and two vertical tubes for missile launching, but two fewer torpedo tubes. Built in 1958 to 1962.

The "Z" class are of large oceangoing type, completed from 1954 to 1960. Their general appearance is very streamlined with a complete row of rapid-flooding holes along the casing. These submarines were stationed in the Baltic and Far East. Mine capacity is alternative to torpedo capacity. All equipped with snort.

The "W" class are a medium-sized type of long-range submarines built from 1950 to 1957, all streamlined, equipped with snort, and fitted for mine-laying. A number are stationed in the Far East. Some units are equipped with a special tank or hangar on deck for carrying guided-missile launchers.

The "Q" class were a new type of medium-range, single screw submarines built from 1954 to 1960 and were improved versions of earlier classes which have been discarded.

	Surface displacement	Submerged displacement	Length	Beam	Draught	Complement
"ZV" class:	2,100 tons	2,600 tons	295 feet	29 feet	19 feet	85
"Z" class:	1,900 tons	2,200 tons	295 feet	26 feet	19 feet	70
"W" class:	1,030 tons	1,180 tons	240 feet	22 feet	15 feet	60
"Q" class:	650 tons	740 tons	185 feet	18 feet	13 feet	40

	Torpedo tubes	Propelling machinery	Shaft horse power	Surface speed	Submerged speed
"ZV" class:	6–21 inch	Diesels/electric motors	10,000/3,500	22 knots	16 knots
"Z" class:	8–21 inch	Diesels/electric motors	10,000/3,500	20 knots	15 knots
"W" class:	6–21 inch	Diesels/electric motors	4,000/2,500	17 knots	15 knots
"Q" class:	4–21 inch	Diesels/electric motors	3,000/2,500	18 knots	16 knots

"Z" Class

"W" Class

LE FORMIDABLE   LE FOUDROYANT   LE REDOUTABLE   LE TERRIBLE

Le Redoutable is the first French nuclear powered ballistic missile armed submarine and the prototype of the "Force Frappe" of four, and possibly five, such vessels which the French Navy plans to have by the late 1970s Their intercontinental ballistic missiles are comparable with the United States "Polaris" weapons, but are of French manufacture with a weight of 15 tons. These submarines have a three months submerged cruise duration, and their diesels have bunkerage for a range of 5,000 miles. *Le Redoutable*, built by Cherbourg Naval Dockyard, was laid down on 30 March 1964 and launched on 29 March 1967 for completion in 1969 and operational service by 1970. *Le Terrible* was begun by the same builders on 24 June 1967 for launching in 1969, and the third unit is in hand. The decision to build a fourth unit of this class was officially announced on 7 December 1967. A tentative name for a fifth vessel is *Implacable*.

Displacement	Length	Beam	Draught	Complement
7,900 tons surface, 9,000 tons submerged	420 feet	34¾ feet	32¾ feet	2 alternating crews of 135

Missile tubes	Torpedo tubes	Propelling machinery	Nuclear reactors	Speed
16 "Polaris" type	4–21 inch	Geared steam turbines	1 pressurised water cooled	20 knots surface, 25 submerged

GYMNOTE

An experimental platform for testing ballistic missiles destined for the first French nuclear powered "Polaris" type submarine, and for use as an underwater laboratory to prove equipment and arms for nuclear submarines: 3,800 tons displacement, 275⅔ ft. length, 34¾ ft. beam, 25 ft. draught, 4 tubes for "Polaris" type ballistic missiles, 2,600 h.p. diesels and electric motors, 2 shafts, speed 11 knots surface and 10 submerged, crew 8 officers and 62 men plus 40 technicians and engineers. Begun at Cherbourg on 17 Mar. 1963, launched on 17 Mar. 1964, completed on 17 Oct. 1966.

Rescindment. The projected nuclear powered fleet submarine, tentatively named *Rubis*, was officially deleted from the list in 1968.

LE REDOUTABLE

GYMNOTE

DAUPHIN	AMAZONE	DAPHNE
ESPADON	ARETHUSE	DIANE
MARSOUIN	ARGONAUTE	DORIS
MORSE	ARIANE	EURYDICE
NARVAL		FLORE
REQUIN		GALATEE
		JUNON
		VENUS

The "Narval" class, completed in 1957–1960, were improved versions of the German XXI type submarines. They were built in seven prefabricated sections each of ten metres in length. *Narval* was first completed without her present bulbous bow. These submarines are being reconstructed and re-engined.

The "Arethuse" class were of a new killer type for hunting submarines. They had a streamlined hull, silent motors, and up-to-date electronic and detection equipment. Completed in 1958–1960.

The "Daphne" class are improved and enlarged versions of the "Arethuse" class, and most successful boats. They were completed from 1964 onwards. Two more units of this type are being built, Psyche and Sirene *Minerva* of this class was lost in the Western Mediterranean on 27 January 1968.

	Surface displacement	Submerged displacement	Length	Beam	Draught
"Narval" class	1,640 tons	1,910 tons	256 feet	23⅔ feet	18 feet
"Arethuse" class:	534 tons	650 tons	164 feet	19 feet	12¾ feet
"Daphne" class:	850 tons	1,040 tons	190¼ feet	22¼ feet	15½ feet

	Torpedo tubes	Propelling machinery	Shaft horse power	Speed	Complement
"Narval" class	8–21.7 inch	Diesels/electric motors	4,000/5,000	16/19 knots	68
"Arethuse" class	4–21.7 inch	Diesels/electric motors	1,060/1,300	16/18 knots	40
"Daphne" class:	12–21.7 inch	Diesels/electric motors	1,300/1,600	13/16 knots	45

Of the five submarines of "La Cérole" class, *L'Africaine* was discarded in 1961, *La Créole* in 1963, *L'Androméde* and *'Astrée* in 1965 and *L'Artémis* in 1966.

DAPHNE

ARIANE

SJOBJORNEN	SJOLEJONET	DELFINEN	NORDKAPAREN	BAVERN	SALEN
SJOHUNDEN	SJOORMEN	DRAKEN	SPRINGAREN	HAJEN	UTTERN
SJOHASTEN		GRIPEN	VARGEN	ILLERN	VALEN

The five new submarines of the "Sjoormen" class completed in 1967–69 are of a highly streamlined long range type, conventionally powered but with engines enabling them to stay submerged for a long time. Five more are in the new construction programme.

The six modern submarines of the "Hajen" class, completed in 1956–60, *Bavern, Hajen, Illern, Salen, Uttern* and *Valen,* are equipped with Schnorkel, and have fast-diving capabilities.

Six more new submarines, *Delfinen, Draken, Gripen, Nordkaparen, Springaren* and *Vargen* were completed in 1961–63; and are also "crash" divers.

There are six surviving coastal submarines, completed in 1943–44, namely *Aborren* (ex-U 5), *Makrillen* (ex-U 9), *Forellen* (ex-U 4), *Laxen* (ex-U 8), *Gaddan* (ex-U 7) and *Siken* (ex-U 6), all of relatively small size, having been designed for operations in the restricted waters of the Baltic. They were reconstructed in 1960–63.

	Surface displacement	*Submerged displacement*	*Length*	*Beam*	*Draught*
"Sjoormen" class:	800 tons	1,110 tons	$167\frac{1}{4}$ feet	20 feet	$19\frac{2}{3}$ feet
"Draken" class:	835 tons	1,000 tons	$227\frac{1}{4}$ feet	$15\frac{3}{4}$ feet	$14\frac{1}{2}$ feet
"Hajen" class:	785 tons	990 tons	$216\frac{1}{4}$ feet	$16\frac{3}{4}$ feet	$19\frac{1}{4}$ feet
"U" class:	430 tons	460 tons	164 feet	$17\frac{1}{2}$ feet	$17\frac{1}{2}$ feet

	Torpedo tubes	*Propelling machinery*	*Shaft horse power*	*Speed*	*Complement*
"Sjoormen" class:	4–21 inch	Diesels/electric motors	1,700/1,700	16/16 knots	50
"Draken" class:	4–21 inch	Diesels/electric motors	1,700/1,700	17/25 knots	50
"Hajen" class:	4–21 inch	Diesels/electric motors	1,700/1,700	16/20 knots	44
"U" class:	4–21 inch	Diesels/electric motors	1,500/750	14/9 knots	23

The nine old submarines of the "Sjolejonet" class were scrapped in 1960–64 and the three old submarines of the "Najad" class were discarded in 1967.

SJOORMEN

HAJEN

CRUISERS

THE term cruiser denoted a self-sufficient fighting ship able to cruise independently half across the world without refuelling, a vessel of high speed, adequate protection and substantial armament which although inferior in fighting power to the battleship was superior to all other types of warships. The main functions of cruisers latterly were to patrol the main ocean highways for the defence of sea-borne trade, to search the outer seas and narrow waters for enemy surface raiders attempting to destroy merchant ships carrying vital cargoes, to destroy merchant ships of the enemy or otherwise interfere with his commerce, to hunt down, bring to action and destroy hostile cruisers or armoured ships known to have escaped from a blockaded port or to be at large, to act as scouts and provide reconnaissance for the main task force at sea, keeping in touch with the enemy and communicating his movements, duties latterly largely taken over by aircraft or reduced by the use of radio and radar, to form a screen against lighter craft when in company with battleships or aircraft carriers, and to carry out the important duty of "showing the Flag". There has always been a wide variation of both displacement and armament within the cruiser category. The generic term cruiser once included all ships not ranked as fighting ships of the line and was applied indiscriminately to frigates, corvettes, sloops and cutters. Later it was used to describe a variety of types ranging from rapid little scouts of 2,000 tons to the monster armoured gun platforms of 14,000 tons, really second-class battleships, which came into the category of cruising ships at the turn of the century. The ultimate development of the armoured cruiser was represented by the *Minotaur, Defence* and *Shannon* of 14,600 tons carrying four 9·2-inch guns and ten 7·5-inch guns at a speed of 23 knots. Formerly cruisers were divided into 1st, 2nd and 3rd classes, but in 1913 the terms cruiser and light cruiser were introduced. In a rapid succession of light cruisers the eight scouts of 2,670 to 2,940 tons with 3-inch guns were succeeded by the four "Town" classes of 4,800 to 5,400 tons with 6-inch guns. The "Arethusa" class of 3,500 tons completed in 1914 were oil fired, with turbines, a speed of $28\frac{1}{2}$ knots, carrying 6-inch and 4·inch guns. The numerically large "C" class of 3,750 to 4,290 tons with four or five 6-inch guns were followed by the "D" class of 4,850 tons with six 6-inch guns and the "E" class of 7,580 tons with seven 6-inch guns and a speed of 33 knots. Meanwhile the semi-heavy cruisers of the "Hawkins" class had appeared with a displacement of 9,770 tons and a main armament of seven 7·5-inch guns. For six years after 1918 no cruisers were laid down. When construction was resumed under the restrictions of the Washington Treaty it resulted in 13 "County" class cruisers of 10,000 tons with eight 8-inch guns and two "City" class cruisers of 8,390 tons with six 8-inch guns. From these heavy cruisers a reversion was made to cruisers of moderate dimensions. The "Leander" and "Perth" classes of 6,830 to 7,270 tons carried eight 6-inch guns and were followed by the altruistically inspired diminutions of the "Arethusa" class of 5,220 tons with six 6-inch guns. In the succeeding group of eight large cruisers of the "Southampton" class the triple turret was introduced for the first time in British cruisers. These, of 9,100 to 9,600 tons, originally mounted twelve 6-inch guns, and were regarded in the fleet as one of the most successful cruiser designs ever produced. These were followed by 16 anti-aircraft light cruisers, eleven of the "Dido" class and five of the Improved "Dido" class, with displacements of 5,770 to 5,900 tons and a main armament of eight or ten 5·25-inch guns. Admiral of the Fleet Earl Jellicoe estimated the number of cruisers necessary for the protection of British seaborne trade to be an absolute minimum of seventy, a figure not attained since 1919. On the outbreak of the Second World War Great Britain had 60 cruisers, but she lost 30 cruisers during the six years of hostilities and she built 30 cruisers under war emergency programmes, so that she still had 60 cruisers at the end of the war. By 1955 these had been reduced to 23 cruisers, and Great Britain had only four cruisers in 1968. There are 35 cruisers in the United States Navy, including three of 17,000 tons, two of 14,700 tons, one nuclear powered and 11 guided missile armed. Soviet Union has 25 cruisers, including 13 of 15,450 tons, and seven guided missile armed.

BLAKE	LION	TIGER

These "Tiger" class cruisers have a remarkable building history. Originally laid down in the middle of the Second World War, they were not launched until the end, when their completion was no longer urgent. Work stopped in July 1946, and they were laid up pending review of their armament. They remained suspended until Oct. 1954, when it was announced they would be resumed, and were dismantled ready for rebuilding to a new design in 1955, being completed in 1959–61 with two of the new fully automatic 6-inch twin turrets in "A" and "Y" positions (instead of three 6-inch turrets in "A", "B" and "Y" positions) and three of the new pattern 3-inch twin turrets one in "B" position and two abreast in "Q" position (instead of ten 40-mm. anti-aircraft guns). In 1965–68 *Blake* was converted with hangar and flight deck abaft the mainmast (the after 6-inch twin turret and the midships two 3 inch twin-turrets having been suppressed). *Tiger* will be similarly converted by 1969 and *Lion* later.

Standard displacement	Full load displacement	Length	Beam	Draught
9,550 tons	12,080 tons	565½ feet	64 feet	22 feet

Guided weapons	Main guns	Secondary guns	Armour	Complement
2 quadruple "Seacat"	2–6 inch	2–3 inch	4 inch	698 to 717

Propelling machinery	Shaft horse power	Boilers	Speed
Parsons geared turbines	80,000	4 Admiralty 3-drum	31·5 knots

Name	No.	Begun	Launched	Completed	Builders and Engineers
BLAKE	C 99	17 Aug. 1942	20 Dec. 1945	8 Mar. 1961	Fairfield S.B. & Eng. Co. Ltd., Govan
LION	C 34	24 June 1942	2 Sept. 1944	20 July 1960	Scotts' S.B. & Eng. Co. Ltd., Greenock *
TIGER	C 20	1 Oct. 1941	25 Oct. 1945	17 Mar. 1959	John Brown & Co. Ltd., Clydebank

*To launching stage. Hull completed by Swan, Hunter & Wigham Richardson, Wallsend, main machinery by Wallsend Slipway & Engineering. The ship built as *Defence* was renamed *Lion* in 1957.

Note. Of the "Colony" class cruisers, *Bermuda* and *Mauritius* were scrapped in 1965 and *Gambia* in 1968. *Sheffield* was scrapped in 1967. *Belfast* is harbour accommodation ship at Portsmouth (Headquarters of Commodore Reserve Ships).

BLAKE

LONG BEACH

The first ship designed and constructed from the keel up as a cruiser for the United States since the end of the Second World War, the first warship armed with a main battery of guided missiles, and the first nuclear-powered surface fighting ship in the world. Designed to operate offensively and independently of other forces under conditions of nuclear warfare, and capable of action against aircraft, guided missiles, surface or sub-surface opposition singly or in support of other forces in both nuclear and non-nuclear warfare. In addition to equipment and weapons for detecting and destroying enemy submarines she carries the United States Navy's modern guided missiles. These include "Talos" and "Terrier", offensive to enemy attack launched from air, sea, land or underwater, whether by missile or conventional assault. The most modern improvements in electronic detection devices were installed in the ship, which projected a radically new picture into future war capabilities. Unlike previous cruisers she has no armour.

Standard displacement	Full load displacement	Length	Beam	Draught
14,200 tons	17,350 tons	721¼ feet	73¼ feet	29 feet

Guided weapons	Anti-submarine weapons	Guns
1 twin "Talos" surface-to-air launcher aft 2 twin "Terrier" surface-to-air launchers forward	ASROC 8-tube launcher amidships 2 triple torpedo launchers	2–5 inch (single) dual purpose

Propelling machinery	Shaft horse power	Nuclear reactors	Speed	Complement
2 geared steam turbines	80,000	2 pressurised water cooled	35 knots	1,020

Name	No.	Begun	Launched	Completed	Builders
LONG BEACH	CGN 9	2 Dec. 1957	14 July 1959	1 Sept. 1961	Bethlehem Steel Co., Quincy, Mass.

LONG BEACH

DES MOINES · NEWPORT NEWS · SALEM

The biggest cruisers ever built, these ships mount the fully automatic 8-inch gun. The large tonnage is accounted for by the extra magazine space required and the great amount of loading and handling gear. The ships were nearly twice the size of contemporary standard British cruisers, with twice the complement. The main armament is capable of a twenty-round-a-minute rate of fire, brass cartridge cases having replaced the old wrapped charges. Whilst capable of delivering an incredible weight of shell in a short time, the ship might be at a disadvantage if a shell hit, disorganised or put out of action the complex loading and fusing mechanism, forcing turret crews to go into local control and manual handling. Superstructure is not so heavy, and they have pole masts, but their great size is emphasised by the fact that they were thirty-seven feet longer than contemporary battleships of the "Indiana" class.

Standard displacement	Full load displacement	Length	Beam	Draught
17,000 tons	21,500 tons	717 feet	76½ feet	26 feet

Main guns	Secondary guns	Anti-aircraft guns	Armour
9–8 inch (3 triple)	12–5 inch dual purpose (6 twin)	8–3 inch (4 twin)	8 inch side, 5 inch deck

Propelling machinery	Shaft horse power	Boilers	Speed	Complement
Geared steam turbines	120,000	4 Babcock & Wilcox	33 knots	1,200 peace; 1,860 war

Name	No.	Begun	Launched	Completed	Builders
DES MOINES	CA 134	28 May 1945	27 Sept. 1946	17 Nov. 1948	Bethlehem Steel Co., Quincy
NEWPORT NEWS	CA 148	1 Oct. 1954	6 Mar. 1947	29 Jan. 1949	Newport News S.B. & D.D. Co.
SALEM	CA 139	4 June 1945	25 Mar. 1947	9 May 1949	Bethlehem Steel Co., Quincy

DES MOINES

ALBANY   CHICAGO   COLUMBUS

Of these fully converted guided missile armed cruisers, *Albany* was originally one of the "Oregon City" class heavy cruisers with one funnel, while *Chicago* and *Columbus* were originally units of the "Baltimore" class heavy cruisers with two funnels, but as both classes otherwise had similar dimensions, armament and propelling machinery and as all three ships were rebuilt to the same design they constitute a homogeneous new class of unique type. The ships were stripped down to the main deck and building to a recast layout started afresh. The reconstruction consisted of the entire suppression of the old conception of armament and separate funnels and masts, and the installation of guided missiles both forward and aft with combined mast-stacks, or "macks", replacing the former masts and stacks. In previous conversions, such as those of *Boston* and *Canberra*, see later page, conventional armament was retained forward while missile launchers were installed aft. *Albany*, *Chicago* and *Columbus* were the first conventionally powered ships to have all guns replaced by missiles, but two 5-inch guns were added subsequently for defence against low aircraft or torpedo boats.

Standard displacement	Full load displacement	Length	Beam	Draught
13,700 tons	17,500 tons	673½ feet	71 feet	27 feet

Guided weapons	Anti-submarine weapons	Guns
2 twin launchers for "Talos" missiles (1 for'd, 1 aft) 2 twin launchers for "Tartar" missiles (1 port, 1 starb'd)	1 octuple rocket launcher	2–5 inch (single) dual-purpose

Propelling machinery	Shaft horse power	Boilers	Speed	Complement
Geared steam turbines	120,000	4 Babcock & Wilcox	33 knots	1,010

Name	No.	Begun	Launched	Completed	Builders	Converted	By
ALBANY	CG 10	6 Mar. 1944	30 June 1945	15 June 1946	Bethlehem Steel	Jan. 59–Nov. 62	Boston N.S.Y.
CHICAGO	CG 11	28 July 1943	20 Aug. 1944	10 Jan. 1945	Philadelphia N.Y.	July 59–Sept. 64	S. Fr'co N.S.Y.
COLUMBUS	CG 12	28 June 1943	30 Nov. 1944	8 June 1945	Bethlehem Steel	June 59–Mar. 63	Puget S.N.S.Y.

ALBANY

OREGON CITY   ROCHESTER

The forerunners of the "Des Moines" class cruisers, these ships incorporated the results of lessons learned during the earlier period of the Second World War in the Pacific, as evidenced by the large close range anti-aircraft battery and arrangements made to control it. The single funnel was adopted to keep as much deck as possible clear for anti-aircraft mountings and to ensure a clear field of fire. *Rochester* was refitted with the new 3-inch anti-aircraft guns in place of her former 40-mm. and 20-mm. anti-aircraft weapons. This was standard replacement procedure in all American warships, as these smaller pieces were considered to be inadequate. As in all American ships refitted for operational service, catapults and fixed-wing aircraft were discarded in *Rochester*; but *Oregon City* retains most of her original armament and equipment. *Albany*, the third ship of this class, was fully converted into a guided-missile cruiser (see previous page).

Standard displacement	Full load displacement	Length	Beam	Draught
13,700 tons	17,500 tons	673½ feet	71 feet	26 feet

Main guns	Secondary guns	Anti-aircraft guns	Armour
9–8 inch	12–5 inch	40–40 mm. (*Oregon City*) 20–3 inch (*Rochester*)	6 inch side, 5 inch deck

Propelling machinery	Shaft horse power	Boilers	Speed	Complement
Geared steam turbines	120,000	4 Babcock & Wilcox	33 knots	1.262

Name	No.	Begun	Launched	Completed	Builders
OREGON CITY	CA 122	8 Apr. 1944	9 Feb. 1945	16 Feb. 1946	Bethlehem Steel Co., Quincy
ROCHESTER	CA 124	29 May 1944	28 Aug. 1945	20 Dec. 1946	Bethlehem Steel Co., Quincy

ROCHESTER

BOSTON   **CANBERRA**

These two ships, originally built as heavy cruisers, were converted into the world's first guided missile cruisers, and they were the first operational combat ships capable of firing supersonic anti-aircraft guided missiles. With their associated radars and guidance systems for the "Terrier" and other anti-aircraft weapons these ships embodied a completely new naval weapons system. During conversion, begun in 1952, the after 8-inch triple gun turret and the after 5-inch twin gun mounting were removed and two twin guided missile launchers were installed on "X" and "Y" positions in their place. Both ships also underwent other drastic changes. The superstructure was entirely remodelled to accommodate the new weapons. One of the original two funnels was removed, vastly altering the appearance of the vessels. The name *Canberra* was a departure from the usual system of nomenclature in United States cruisers: originally named *Pittsburgh*, just before completion she was re-named in commemoration of an Australian cruiser, H.M.A.S. *Canberra*, which was sunk in the First Battle of Savo Island on 9 August 1942.

Standard displacement	*Full load displacement*	*Length*	*Beam*	*Draught*
13,300 tons	17,500 tons	673½ feet	71 feet	26 feet
Guided weapons	*Main guns*	*Secondary guns*	*Anti-aircraft guns*	*Armour*
2 twin launchers for	6–8 inch	10–5 inch	8–3 inch	6 inch side,
"Terrier" weapons (aft)	(2 triple) forward	(5 twin)	(4 twin)	3 inch decks
Propelling machinery	*Shaft horse power*	*Boilers*	*Speed*	*Complement*
Geared steam turbines	120,000	4 Babcock & Wilcox	34 knots	1,273

Name	No.	Begun	Launched	Completed	Builders	Converted	By
BOSTON	CA 69	30 June 1941	26 May 1942	30 June 1943	Bethlehem Steel	1 Nov. 1955	New York S.B. Corp.
CANBERRA	CA 70	3 Sept. 1941	19 Apr. 1943	14 Oct. 1943	Bethlehem Steel	15 June 1956	New York S.B. Corp

BOSTON

| BALTIMORE | FALL RIVER | LOS ANGELES | PITTSBURGH | ST. PAUL |
| BREMERTON | HELENA | MACON | QUINCY | TOLEDO |

The standard American heavy cruiser of the Second World War. A number of other hulls of this class were converted into aircraft carriers prior to their launch. Two ships, *Boston* and *Canberra*, had their after turrets removed and replaced by "Terrier" guided-missile launchers in 1952–56 (see previous page). *Helena, Los Angeles, Macon* and *Toledo* were formerly fitted to carry "Regulus" guided missiles, but with little change in previous armament and they were not classed as guided missile cruisers. In all activated units 40-mm. mounts were replaced by twenty (subsequently reduced to twelve or fourteen) 3-inch guns in twin mounts. Two other ships of this class were taken in hand for complete conversion to guided-missile cruisers in 1959, namely *Chicago* and *Columbus* (previous page). They have "Talos" surface-to-air missiles mounted in twin launchers fore and aft and "Tartar" launchers installed amidships. Nos. CA 68, 130, 131, 75, 135, 132, 72, 71, 73 and 133, respectively, in alphabetical order of names above.

Standard displacement	Full load displacement	Length	Beam	Draught
13,600 tons	17,200 tons	673½ feet	71 feet	26 feet

Main guns	Secondary guns	Anti-aircraft guns	Aircraft	Armour
9–8 inch	10–5 inch	12 or 14–3 inch	1 helicopter	6 inch side, 5 inch deck

Propelling machinery	Shaft horse power	Boilers	Speed	Complement
Geared steam turbines	120,000	4 Babcock & Wilcox	33 knots	1,146

Note: Baltimore, Quincy, Pittsburgh, St. Paul and Helena were built by Bethlehem Steel Co., Quincy; *Bremerton, Fall River, Macon* and *Toledo* by New York Shipbuilding Corporation; *Los Angeles* by Philadelphia Navy Yard. All completed in this order of names for each yard between April 1943 and October 1946.

ST. PAUL

ROANOKE   **WORCESTER**

The largest American so-called "light" cruisers, these vessels reverted to the twin turret, unusual for American design. Armed with 6-inch guns they were, by Treaty definition, "light" cruisers even though in tonnage they exceeded the displacement of the majority of the world's heavy cruisers. Eight intended sisters to these ships were cancelled at the end of the Second World War, two actually having been commenced. The main armament is semi-automatic and can be used as an anti-aircraft battery. Gun layout, and indeed the general design of the ships, was similar to that of the contemporary anti-aircraft cruisers of the "Juneau" class for which at a distance they could easily have been mistaken.

Standard displacement	Full load displacement	Length	Beam	Draught
14,700 tons	18,500 tons	679½ feet	70⅔ feet	25 feet

Main guns	Secondary guns	Armour	Complement
12–6 inch	24–3 inch (*Roanoke*), 12–3 inch (*Worcester*)	6 inch side, 5 inch deck	1,170 peace, 1,700 war

Propelling machinery	Shaft horse power	Boilers	Speed
Geared steam turbines	120,000	4 Babcock & Wilcox	32 knots

Name	No.	Begun	Launched	Completed	Builders
ROANOKE	CA 145	15 May 1945	16 June 1947	4 Apr. 1948	New York Shipbuilding Corporation
WORCESTER	CA 144	29 Jan. 1945	4 Feb. 1947	25 June 1948	New York Shipbuilding Corporation

Note. Of the two single funnelled large "light" cruisers of the "Fargo" class (see 1960 Edition, page 80), *Huntington* was stricken from the Navy List in 1962 and *Fargo* is out of commission in reserve. (10,500 tons standard, 14,055 tons full load; 12–6 inch guns, 12–5 inch guns.)

The small anti-aircraft cruisers of the "Juneau" class (see 1960 Edition, page 84) were scrapped "stricken") in 1959–66.

WORCESTER

GALVESTON   LITTLE ROCK   OKLAHOMA CITY   PROVIDENCE   SPRINGFIELD   TOPEKA

These six former so-called "light" cruisers of the "Cleveland" class (which were nevertheless big enough for some to be completed as aircraft carriers) were converted into guided missile cruisers. They have conventional armament forward and amidships, and guided missile launchers aft, three being armed with "Talos" missiles and three with "Terrier" missiles. *Little Rock, Oklahoma City, Providence* and *Springfield* were refitted as flagships, the navigating bridge and forward superstructure being reconstructed to provide for flag spaces and to include high frequency radio systems with side band capability. Other work, such as improvements in habitability, was also done in conjunction with the installation of missile systems. In appearance these ships vary considerably: *Galveston*, with two lattice masts differs from *Topeka* with a tripod foremast and lattice mainmast and mizzenmast; and both ships differ from *Providence* and *Springfield*, sister ships with three lattice masts, which again differ from *Little Rock* and *Oklahoma City* with two lattice masts.

Standard displacement	Full load displacement	Length	Beam	Draught
10,670 tons	14,600 tons	610 feet	66⅔ feet	25 feet

Guided weapons	Main guns	Secondary guns	Armour
1 twin launcher aft for	6–6 inch (2 triple)	6–5 inch (3 twin)	5 inch belts
"Talos" missiles (*Gal., L.R., O.C.*)	*Galveston, Topeka*	*Galveston, Topeka*	5 inch decks
"Terrier" missiles (*Pro., Spr., Top.*)	3–6 inch (1 triple)	2–5 inch (1 twin)	
	L.R., O.C., P. and *S.*	*L.R., O.C., P.* and *S.*	

Propelling machinery	Shaft horse power	Boilers	Speed	Complement
Geared steam turbines	100,000	4 Babcock & Wilcox	31½ knots	1,200 (flagships, 1,680)

Name	No.	Begun	Launched	Completed	Builders	Converted	By
GALVESTON	CLG 3	20 Feb. 44	22 Apr. 45	25 May 46	Cramp S.B. Co.	Aug. 56–Sept. 58	Philadelphia N.S.Y.
LITTLE ROCK	CLG 4	6 Mar. 43	27 Aug. 44	17 June 45	Cramp S.B. Co.	Jan. 57–June 60	New York S.B. Corp.
OKLAHOMA CITY	CLG 5	8 Mar. 42	20 Feb. 44	22 Dec. 44	Cramp S.B. Co.	May 57–Sept. 60	Beth. S. Co. S. Fr'co.
PROVIDENCE	CLG 6	27 July 43	28 Dec. 44	15 May 45	Bethlehem, Qu.	June 57–Sept. 59	Boston Naval S.Y.
SPRINGFIELD	CLG 7	13 Feb. 43	9 Mar. 44	8 Sept. 44	Bethlehem, Qu.	Aug. 57–July 60	Beth. S. Co., Quincy
TOPEKA	CLG 8	21 Apr. 43	19 Aug. 44	23 Dec. 44	Bethlehem, Qu.	Aug. 57–Mar. 60	New York N.S.Y.

LITTLE ROCK

AMSTERDAM   ASTORIA   PASADENA   PORTSMOUTH   WILKES-BARRE

Although classed as light cruisers on account of their 6-inch guns, these ships of the "Cleveland" class are larger than many heavy cruisers of the pre-war era. Numerically the largest class ever ordered, 27 were completed as cruisers and nine were converted into aircraft carriers. Typically American in appearance; with raking pole masts and tall funnels set close together, they could be mistaken for the "Baltimore" class heavy cruisers in a hasty observation. In 1958–60 *Galveston, Little Rock, Oklahoma City, Providence, Springfield* and *Topeka* of this class (see previous page) were converted into guided-missile cruisers, with twin launchers aft. *Atlanta* of this class was converted into an experimental target ship in 1964.

Standard displacement	Full load displacement	Length	Beam	Draught
10,500 tons	13,755 tons	610 feet	66 feet	25 feet

Main guns	Secondary guns	Anti-aircraft guns	Armour
12–6 inch	12–5 inch	28–40 mm.	5 inch side, 3 inch deck

Propelling machinery	Shaft horse power	Boilers	Speed	Complement
Geared steam turbines	100,000	4 Babcock & Wilcox	33 knots	916

Name	No.	Begun	Launched	Completed	Builders
AMSTERDAM	CL 101	3 Mar. 1943	25 Apr. 1944	8 Jan. 1945	Newport News S.B. & D.D. Co.
ASTORIA	CL 90	6 Sept. 1941	6 Mar. 1943	17 May 1944	Cramp Shipbuilding Co.
PASADENA	CL 65	6 Feb. 1943	28 Dec. 1943	8 June 1944	Bethlehem Steel Co., Quincy
PORTSMOUTH	CL 102	15 Dec. 1941	28 June 1943	25 June 1945	Newport News S.B. & D.D. Co.
WILKES-BARRE	CL 103	14 Dec. 1942	24 Dec. 1943	1 July 1944	New York Shipbuilding Corp.

Note: Birmingham, Cleveland, Columbia, Denver, Houston, Mobile, Montpelier and *Santa Fe* of the above class were scrapped in 1959, *Dulath* and *Manchester* were stricken in 1960; *Biloxi, Dayton* and *Miami* in 1961; *Vicksburg* in 1962; *Vincennes* in 1966.

PORTSMOUTH

ADMIRAL LAZAREV	ALEKSANDR NYEVSKI	DZERKHINSKI	OKTYABRSKAYA
ADMIRAL NAKHIMOV	ALEKSANDR SUVOROV	MIKHAIL KUTUZOV	REVOLUTSIYA
ADMIRAL SENYAVIN	DMITRI POZHARSKY	MURMANSK	SVERDLOV
ADMIRAL USHAKOV			ZHDANOV

Among the most powerful conventional cruisers afloat, little was known of these ships until 1953, when *Sverdlov* attended the Coronation Review at Spithead, and one of her sisters paid a courtesy visit to Sweden. It is believed that seventeen hulls were launched from 1951 onwards, but only fourteen ships were completed. There is slight variation in later ships in the siting of the anti-aircraft mountings. There is an armour belt around the whole hull, of at least four-inch thickness. Two sets of mine rails were fitted on the quarterdeck. The secondary armament turrets are very similar to the German 4.1-inch mounts with the guns mounted very far back in the turret and elevating in the roof rather than the turret face. To be distinguished from "Chapayev" class by break of forecastle deck being abaft the after superstructure, not abreast the forefunnel. All these ships were originally designed for a displacement of 12,800 tons standard and 17,000 tons full load. *Molotovsk* was renamed *Oktyabrskaya Revolutsiya* in 1957.

Standard displacement 15,450 tons	*Full load displacement* 19,200 tons	*Length* 689 feet	*Beam* 70 feet	*Draught* 24½ feet
Main guns 12–5·9 inch	*Secondary guns* 12–3·9 inch	*Anti-aircraft guns* 32–37 mm.	*Torpedo tubes* 10–21 inch	*Mines* 140 to 250
Propelling machinery Geared steam turbines	*Shaft horse power* 130,000	*Boilers* 4	*Speed* 34 knots	*Complement* 1,050

Note. Of this "Sverdlov" class *Ordzhonikidze* was transferred to the Indonesian Navy in 1962 and renamed *Irian*.

ZHDANOV

KOMSOMOLETS   KUIBYSHEV   ZHELEZNYAKOV

Designed as a logical development of the original "Kirov" type, the construction of these cruisers of the "Chapayev" class, begun in 1939–40, had to be stopped during the Second World War, and they were not resumed until 1946 and 1947. In several respects they resemble their successors of the "Sverdlov" class, but the forecastle deck level breaks just abaft the forefunnel instead of right aft at the quarter deck. They also have a somewhat more built-up appearance abaft the funnels which are vertical instead of raked as in the "Kirov" class. They were launched during 1941–47 and completed in 1948–50. The catapults originally mounted were subsequently removed from all the ships of this type. Their turret guns are in separate sleeves allowing the main armament independent elevation which is at least 50 degrees. The ships have a heavy director on the control tower, a pole foremast and a tripod mainmast forward of the after funnel. All this class have higher freeboard and taller funnels than the cruisers of the "Kirov" class. They have auxiliary diesel motors for cruising speeds in addition to the main geared steam turbines. The cruiser of this class originally named *Chkalov* was renamed *Komsomolets* in 1961. *Zheleznyakov* serves as a training ship. *Frunse* and *Chapayev* of this class were discarded for disposal, the latter having been dismantled in 1961.

Standard displacement	Full load displacement	Length	Beam	Draught
11,500 tons	15,000 tons	656 feet	64¾ feet	21 feet

Main guns	Secondary guns	Anti-aircraft guns	Mines	Armour
12–6 inch	8–4 inch	28–37 mm.	100 to 200	Heavy side belt

Propelling machinery	Shaft horse power	Boilers	Speed	Complement
Geared steam turbines and cruising diesels	113,000	6	35 knots	834

ZHELEZNYAKOV

KALININ   **KIROV**   **SLAVA**

The first class of cruisers built for the Soviet Navy since the Revolution, these ships are said to have been designed by Italian experts, a belief certainly not belied by their appearance. Originally the class comprised six heavy cruisers (heavy by virtue of their main armament) falling into two groups of four and two ships, but all the vessels had similar armament and dimensions. The triple guns are mounted in one sleeve and are incapable of individual elevation. The maximum elevation is 40 degrees. Two sister ships were destroyed incomplete on the slip at the time of the German invasion and three were recently disposed of. One vessel had a long refit, making her recognitionally somewhat similar to the later "Chapayev" and "Sverdlov" types. *Molotov* was renamed *Slava* in 1962. Of this class, *Voroshilov* was scrapped, *Kaganovitch* was lent or leased by Soviet Union to the Chinese Communist Navy, *Maksim Gorki* was disarmed and in a bad state, and *Kalinin* and *Slava* were latterly little more than training hulks. *Kalinin* recently served under the name *Petropavlovsk*. Details of the surviving "Kirov" class ships are given below, but for her role as a training ship *Kirov* herself mounts nine 7.1-inch guns, six 3.9 inch guns, eight 37 mm. guns, two older guns and no torpedo tubes.

Standard displacement	*Full load displacement*	*Length*	*Beam*	*Draught*
8,800 tons	11,500 tons	626¾ feet	59 feet	20 feet

Main guns	*Secondary guns*	*Anti-aircraft guns*	*Torpedo tubes*	*Mines*
9–7.1 inch (3 triple)	8–4 inch (4 twin)	16–37 mm., 6–13 mm.	6–21 inch	60 to 90

Propelling machinery	*Shaft horse power*	*Boilers*	*Speed*	*Complement*
Geared steam turbines and cruising diesels	110,000	6 Yarrow or Normand	34 knots	734

KIROV

COLBERT   DE GRASSE

De Grasse, ordered under the 1937 Estimates, was suspended during the German occupation of Lorient, but her construction was resumed in 1946 until her launch when building stopped pending the study of anti-aircraft equipment, and owing to financial stringency. Work was again continued on 9 Jan. 1951, and she was completed to a modified design as an anti-aircraft cruiser in Brest Dockyard, with revised armament. She is equipped as a fleet command ship, and for radar control of air strikes.

Colbert is of improved "De Grasse" type. Provision was made in her design so that she can be fitted eventually with guided missiles. She has a scheme of protection quite different from that of her half-sister, and has a platform for a helicopter. As a fast transport she could carry 2,400 officers and men with full equipment. Her guns are radar controlled with stabilised gunlayers for automatic tracking.

Standard displacement	Full load displacement	Length	Beam	Draught
Colbert 9,080 tons	11,100 tons	593¼ feet	64⅔ feet	25 feet
De Grasse 10,238 tons	12,350 tons	620 feet	61 feet	21½ feet

Main guns	Secondary guns	Armour	Aircraft	Complement
16–5 inch	20–57 mm	4 inch side, 3 inch deck	1 helicopter	777 peace, 964 war
12–5 inch	removed	(*De Grasse*)	(*Colbert*)	651 peace, 952 war

Propelling machinery	Shaft horse power	Boilers	Speed
Geared steam turbines	86,000	4	32 knots
Geared steam turbines	105,000	4	33·5 knots

Name	No.	Begun	Launched	Completed	Builders
COLBERT	C 611	Dec. 1953	24 Mar. 1959	5 May 1959	Brest Dockyard
DE GRASSE	C 610	Nov. 1938	11 Sept. 1946	3 Sept. 1956	Lorient and Brest Dockyard

COLBERT

VITTORIO VENETO

A unique multi-purpose guided missile armed cruiser and helicopter carrier of sophisticated and compact design, *Vittorio Veneto* is a beamy vessel developed from the basic plans of the guided missile escort cruisers of the Andrea Doria" class, but with provision made for considerable strengthening of the helicopter squadron and improved facilities for anti-submarine warfare operations. The ship was originally projected under the 1959–1960 new construction programme as a third unit of the "Andrea Doria" class but her design was subsequently recast several times in the light of revised fleet requirements to incorporate scaled-up improvements and later pattern equipment. A considerable proportion of her length aft is devoted to aircraft operations where provision is made for a substantial flight deck for no fewer than nine A/B 240B ASW helicopters. Her boilers work at a pressure of 711 pounds per square inch and a temperature of 842 degrees Fahrenheit. With a capacity of 1,200 tons of oil fuel she has a radius of action of 6,000 miles at a speed of 20 knots. She was to have had a sister ship, but *Trieste* (ex-*Italia*) will be of different design and probably an entirely new category.

Standard displacement	Full load displacement	Length	Beam	Draught
7,500 tons	8,850 tons	557¾ feet	63⅜ feet	17¼ feet

Guided weapons	Main and A.A. Guns	Torpedo tubes	Aircraft
1 twin launcher for "Terrier" missiles	8–3 inch dual purpose	2 triple for A/S	9 helicopters

Propelling machinery	Shaft horse power	Boilers	Speed	Complement
Geared steam turbines	73,000	4 Foster Wheeler	32 knots	550

Name	No.	Begun	Launched	Completion	Builders
VITTORIO VENETO	C 550	10 June 1965	5 Feb. 1967	1968–1969	Navalmeccanica, Castellammare di Stabia

VITTORIO VENETO

GIUSEPPE GARIBALDI

The sole survivor of the once large pre-war Italian cruiser force, *Giuseppe Garibaldi* was converted into a guided-missile cruiser with a twin "Terrier" launcher aft. Her appearance was completely altered, with a single large trunked funnel (in place of two funnels) and lattice masts. She was commissioned for operational service in 1962. In addition to the guided weapons, the new armament includes four 5.3-inch dual purpose guns of a new fully automatic model disposed in two twin turrets forward, and an anti-aircraft battery of eight 3-inch fully automatic weapons, also of a new pattern, built by O.T.O. La Spezia, disposed in single turrets, four on each side amidships abreast the funnel and the bridge, with a rate of fire of 57 rounds per minute. On her original trials, when the ship was first built, she developed 104,030 shaft horse power and attained a speed of 33.6 knots. During reconstruction her machinery was completely refitted. She was originally a sister ship of the light cruiser *Luigi di Savoia Duca degli Abruzzi* which was removed from the effective list in 1961.

Standard displacement	Full load displacement	Length	Beam	Draught
9,802 tons	11,335 tons	613½ feet	61⅔ feet	22 feet

Guided weapons		Main guns	Anti-aircraft guns	Armour
4 tubes aft for ballistic missiles		4–5.3 inch (2 twin)	8–3 inch (single)	4½ inch side
1 twin launcher aft for "Terrier" missiles				

Propelling machinery	Shaft horse power	Boilers	Speed	Complement
Geared steam turbines	100,000	6 of 3-drum type	30 knots	694

Name	No.	Begun	Launched	Completed	Builders	Converted
GIUSEPPE GARIBALDI	C 551	Dec. 1933	21 Apr. 1936	Dec. 1937	C. R. dell' Adriatico	1957–1962

Note. The cadets' training cruiser *Raimondo Montecuccoli* was scrapped in 1964.

GIUSEPPE GARIBALDI

DE RUYTER   ### DE ZEVEN PROVINCIEN

Bearing the names of famous warships of the past, and, incidentally, that of one another, their names having been transposed, these ships represented the latest in European cruiser design. Laid down in 1939 their hulls were captured by the Germans and intermittent work continued. The present *De Ruyter* was launched by the Germans, but as *De Zeven Provincien*. Somewhat American in design, the secondary armament is superimposed over the main armament. All guns are fully automatic and radar controlled. The remarkable combined mast and funnel design was unique among the world's cruisers. The mainmast was originally abaft the after funnel, but it was subsequently stepped before the after funnel, doubtless because heat and smoke affected the radar gear. The shape of the bow differs in the two ships, which accounts for the variations in the overall lengths. During her conversion in 1962–64 the after turrets of *De Zeven Provincien* were replaced with guided-missile launching equipment, and a separate mainmast again appeared abaft the after funnel.

	Standard displacement	*Full load displacement*	*Length*	*Beam*	*Draught*
De Ruyter:	9,529 tons	11,850 tons	614½ feet	57 feet	22 feet
De 7 Prov:	9,850 tons	12.250 tons	609 feet		

	Guided weapons	*Main guns*	*Secondary guns*	*Anti-aircraft guns*	*Armour*
De Ruyter:	1 twin launcher for "Terrier" missiles	8–6 inch	8–57 mm.	8–40 mm.	3 inch side
De 7 Prov:	(in *De Zeven Provincien* only)	4–6 inch	6–57 mm.	4–40 mm.	

Propelling machinery	*Shaft horse power*	*Boilers*	*Speed*	*Complement*
Parsons geared steam turbines	85,000	4 of 3-drum type	32 knots	926 De R.; 940 De 7 P.

Name	*No.*	*Begun*	*Launched*	*Completed*	*Builders*
DE RUYTER	C 801	5 Sept. 1939	24 Dec. 1944	18 Nov. 1953	Wilton-Fijenoord, Schiedam
DE ZEVEN PROVINCIEN	C 802	19 May 1939	22 Aug. 1950	17 Dec. 1953	Rotterdam Drydock Co.

DE ZEVEN PROVINCIEN

GÖTA LEJON

The Royal Swedish Navy's only remaining heavy ship, this cruiser cannot be mistaken for any other ship, an enormous director on a box bridge, light tripod masts and very heavily raked, squat funnels being her recognition features. An unusual gun arrangement with a triple turret forward and two twin turrets aft also marks her out. The 6-inch guns are high angle anti-aircraft weapons with an elevation of 70 degrees and are automatic and dual purpose. The ship now has an enclosed tower bridge structure. So large is the bridge in comparison to the forward turret that at a distance the ship does not seem to mount a forward armament. *Göta Lejon* and her sister ship *Tre Kronor* were reconstructed and refitted in 1951–52, when the nine 25-mm. anti-aircraft pieces formerly mounted were suppressed and seven 40-mm. anti-aircraft guns added. *Göta Lejon* was modernised in 1958, with new radar and 57-mm guns among other features; but *Tre Kronor* was discarded in 1964.

Standard displacement	Full load displacement	Length	Beam	Draught
8,200 tons	9,200 tons	597 feet	54 feet	21½ feet

Main guns	Anti-aircraft guns	Torpedo tubes	Mines	Armour
7–6 inch	4–57 mm.; 11–40 mm.	6–21 inch	120	5 inch side

Propelling machinery	Shaft horse power	Boilers	Speed	Complement
De Laval geared steam turbines	100,000	4 of 4-drum type	33 knots	610

Name	Begun	Launched	Completed	Builders
GÖTA LEJON	27 Sept. 1943	17 Nov. 1945	15 Dec. 1947	Eriksberg, Mekaniska Verkstad, Göteberg

Note: The cadets' seagoing training cruiser *Gotland*, formerly an anti-aircraft cruiser, and before that a cruiser seaplane carrier, was sold in 1961.

GÖTA EJON

CANARIAS

Designed by a former Director of Naval Construction in the Royal Navy, and projected on the basic pattern of the contemporary British heavy cruisers of the later "County" class, this ship is unique among the world's cruisers in that she reverted to a twenty-five year-old design. From her launching until her refit in 1952–3 she was distinguished by an enormous single-trunked funnel, but she was rebuilt to her original design of twin funnels, a reversal of the usual procedure. Heavy turrets, massive bridge tower, and absence of funnel rake readily identify her. The maximum elevation of her 8-inch guns is 70 degrees. She is named after the Canary Islands. Her sister ship *Baleares*, was torpedoed and sunk in March 1938 during the Spanish Civil War.

Standard displacement	Full load displacement	Length	Beam	Draught
10,670 tons	13,500 tons	636½ feet	64 feet	21⅓ feet

Main guns	Secondary guns	Anti-aircraft guns	Torpedo tubes	Armour
8–8 inch	8–4.7 inch	4–37 mm., 2–20 mm.	(12–21 inch removed)	2 inch side

Propelling machinery	Shaft horse power	Boilers	Speed	Complement
Geared steam turbines	92,000	8 Yarrow	31 knots	1,022

Name		Begun	Launched	Completed	Builders
CANARIAS	C 21	15 Aug. 1928	28 May 1931	1 Oct. 1936	Sociedad Espanola de Construccion Naval, El Ferrol

Note: The old light cruisers of the "Galicia" class, *Almirante Cervera*, *Galicia* and *Miguel de Cervantes*, were stricken from the Navy List in 1966.

The old anti-aircraft light cruiser *Méndez Nuñez* was stricken in 1963, and the obsolete light cruiser *Navarra* in 1956.

CANARIAS

GENERAL BELGRANO	BARROSO	O'HIGGINS
NUEVE DE JULIO	TAMANDARE	PRAT

Formerly United States large light cruisers of the "Brooklyn" class, these ships became the Argentinian *General Belgrano* (ex-17 *de Octubre*, ex-U.S.S. *Phoenix*) and 9 *de Julio* (ex-U.S.S. *Boise*), Brazilian *Barroso* (ex-U.S.S. *Philadelphia*) and *Tamandare* (es-U.S.S. *St. Louis*), and Chilean *Prat* (ex-U.S.S. *Nashville*) and *O'Higgins* (ex-U.S.S. *Brooklyn*). All were transferred in 1951 as part of a plan to strengthen South American navies. The ships are of somewhat unusual appearance, with a lattice tower between the funnels, a considerable gap between the after funnel and mainmast, and the third triple turret forward at main-deck level trained aft.

Standard displacement	Full load displacement	Length	Beam	Draught
9,700 to 10,800 tons	13,000 to 13,645 tons	608½ feet	69 feet	24 feet

Main guns	Secondary guns	Anti-aircraft guns	Aircraft	Armour
15–6 inch	8–5 inch	28–40 mm., 8 to 24–20 mm.	1 or 2 helicopters	4 inch side, 5 inch deck

Propelling machinery	Shaft horse power	Boilers	Speed	Complement
Geared steam turbines	100,000	8 Babcock & Wilcox	32.5 knots	888 to 1,200

Name	No.	Begun	Launched	Completed	Builders
GENERAL BELGRANO	4	15 Apr. 1935	12 Mar. 1938	18 Mar. 1939	New York Shipbuilding Corp.
NUEVO DE JULIO	5	1 Apr. 1935	3 Dec. 1936	1 Feb. 1939	Newport News Shipbuilding Co.
BARROSO	C 11	28 May 1935	17 Nov. 1936	28 July 1938	Philadelphia Navy Yard
TAMANDARE	C 12	10 Dec. 1936	15 Apr. 1938	10 Dec. 1939	Newport News Shipbuilding Co.
O'HIGGINS	CL 02	12 Mar. 1935	30 Nov. 1936	18 July 1938	New York Navy Yard
PRAT	CL 03	24 Jan. 1935	2 Oct. 1937	25 Nov. 1938	New York Shipbuilding Corp.

Note: Argentina also has the training cruiser *La Argentina*, completed in 1939, with a displacement of 6,000 tons, a main armament of nine 6-inch guns, and a speed of 30 knots (see full particulars on page 102 of the 1960 Edition); but her two old heavy cruisers *Almirante Brown* and *Veinticinco de Mayo* were scrapped in 1962.

TAMANDARE

ALMIRANTE GRAU   CORONEL BOLOGNESI

These two former British cruisers represent successive developments of the "Colony" class, with "X" turret suppressed and anti-aircraft armament augmented. *Newfoundland* was fitted with two new pattern lattice masts, but *Ceylon* was refitted with lattice foremast only and retained her tripod mainmast. The six torpedo tubes were removed from both vessels. H.M.S. *Newfoundland* was purchased by the Peruvian Government on 2 Nov. 1959 and formally transferred to the Peruvian Navy at Portsmouth on 30 Dec. 1959 and renamed *Almirante Grau*. H.M.S. *Ceylon* was purchased by Peru (announced 18 Dec. 1959) and formally transferred to the Peruvian Navy at Portsmouth on 9 Feb. 1960 and renamed *Coronel Bolognesi*.

	Standard displacement	Full load displacement	Length	Beam	Draught
Almirante Grau:	8,800 tons	11,110 tons	555½ feet	63⅜ feet	21 feet
Coronel Bolognesi:	8,781 tons	11,090 tons			

Main guns	Secondary guns	Anti-aircraft guns	Armour	Complement
9–6 inch	8–4 inch	12–40 mm. (A.G.)	4 inch	743 (A.G.)
		18–40 mm. (C.B.)		766 (C.B.)

Propelling machinery	Shaft horse power	Boilers	Speed
Geared steam turbines	72,500	4 Admiralty 3-drum type	31.5 knots

Name	No.	Begun	Launched	Completed	Builders
ALMIRANTE GRAU	81	9 Nov. 1939	19 Dec. 1941	31 Dec. 1942	Swan, Hunter & Wigham Richardson, Tyne
CORONEL BOLOGNESI	82	27 Apr. 1939	30 July 1942	13 July 1943	Alex. Stephen & Sons, Ltd., Govan, Glasgow

ALMIRANTE GRAU

MYSORE

Formerly H.M.S. *Nigeria* of the British "Colony" class, her purchase from Great Britain for the Indian Navy was announced on 8 April, 1954. She underwent an extensive refit and conversion at the Birkenhead Shipyard of Cammell Laird & Co. Ltd., before commissioning for operational service. The ship originally had four triple 6-inch turrets, two forward and two aft, and two tripod masts. During reconstruction her triple 6-inch turret in "X" position and her two triple banks of 21-inch torpedo tubes were removed and two lattice masts were stepped. Her bridge was modified as in the British *Newfoundland*, all electrical equipment was replaced, the propelling machinery was overhauled, and various parts of the ship extensively modified. The ship was formally handed over to the Indian Navy at Birkenhead and renamed *Mysore* on 29 Aug. 1957.

Standard displacement	Full load displacement	Length	Beam	Draught
8,700 tons	11,040 tons	555½ feet	62 feet	21 feet

Main guns	Secondary guns	Anti-aircraft guns	Armour	Complement
9–6 inch	8–4 inch	12–40 mm.	4½ inch	800

Propelling machinery	Shaft horse power	Boilers	Speed
Geared steam turbines	72,500	4 Admiralty 3-drum type	31.5 knots

Name	No.	Begun	Launched	Completed	Builders
MYSORE	C 60	8 Feb. 1938	18 July 1939	23 Sept. 1940	Vickers-Armstrongs Ltd., Tyne

Note: India also has the old light cruiser *Delhi* (ex-H.M.S. *Achilles*), C 74, completed in 1933, with a displacement of 7,114 tons, a main armament of six 6-inch guns, and a speed of 32 knots (see full particulars and photograph on pages 110 and 111 of the 1960 Edition).

MYSORE

BABUR

This ship, formerly H.M.S. *Diadem* of the Royal Navy, is one of the anti-aircraft light cruisers built under the Second World War estimates. The Admiralty announced the sale of the vessel to Pakistan on 29 February 1956. She was refitted in H.M. Dockyard, Portsmouth, in 1957 with new radar, two whip aerials on the bridge and revised secondary armament, and officially turned over to the Pakistan Navy at Portsmouth on 5 July 1957 and renamed *Babur* after the founder of the great Mogul Empire (*Diadem* means the emblem of sovereignty). She was converted into a cadet training ship in 1961. She belonged to the Improved "Dido" class of which *Bellona* was scrapped in 1959, *Black Prince* in 1962 and *Royalist* in 1966 (both the latter were in the Royal New Zealand Navy), and *Spartan* was a Second World War loss. (Of the eleven ships of the original "Dido" class, *Bonaventure*, *Charybdis*, *Hermione* and *Naiad* were Second World War losses, *Scylla* was broken up in 1950, *Argonaut*, *Phoebe* and *Sirius* were scrapped in 1955–56, and *Cleopatra*, *Dido* and *Euryalus* went to the shipbreakers in 1958–59.)

Standard displacement	Full load displacement	Length	Beam	Draught
5,900 tons	7,560 tons	512 feet	52 feet	18½ feet

Main guns	Anti-aircraft guns	Torpedo tubes	Armour
8–5.25 inch dual purpose	14–40 mm.	6–21 inch (tripled)	3 inch

Propelling machinery	Shaft horse power	Boilers	Speed	Complement
Geared steam turbines	62,000	4 Admiralty 3-drum type	32 knots	588

Name	No.	Begun	Launched	Completed	Builders
BABUR	84	15 Nov. 1939	26 Aug. 1942	6 Jan. 1944	R. & W. Hawthorn Leslie & Co., Ltd., Hebburn-on-Tyne

BABUR

ANTRIM	FIFE	HAMPSHIRE	LONDON
DEVONSHIRE	**GLAMORGAN**	**KENT**	**NORFOLK**

Projected as fleet escorts and designed to embody the latest developments in the destroyer field. It was found later possible to arm them with guided weapons instead of anti-aircraft guns. They eventually materialised as an entirely new design and of so novel a type, stemming from but far in advance of and considerably bigger than destroyers, as to constitute a new category. The helicopter is served by a hangar and flight apron at the after end of the upper deck. Each shaft set of the twin screw main propulsion plant consists of a high and low pressure steam turbine of 15,000 s.h.p. combined output plus two gas turbines each developing 7,500 s.h.p. Of handsome and symmetrical appearance, their construction and layout reflect great ingenuity.

Standard displacement	Full load displacement	Length	Beam	Draught
5,200 tons	6,200 tons	520½ feet	54 feet	20 feet

Guided missiles	Guns	Aircraft	Anti-submarine weapons
1 twin launcher for "Seaslug" missiles	4–4.5 inch (2 twin)	Wessex	2 homing torpedoes
2 quadruple launchers for "Seacat" missiles	2–20 mm. (single)	Helicopter	dropped by helicopter

Propelling machinery	Shaft horse power	Boilers	Speed	Complement
Combined steam and gas turbines	60,000	2 Babcock & Wilcox	32.5 knots	471

Name	No.	Begun	Launched	Completed	Builders
ANTRIM	D 18	20 Jan. 1966	19 Oct. 1967		Fairfield Shipbuilding & Eng., Govan
DEVONSHIRE	D 02	9 Mar. 1959	10 June 1960	15 Nov. 1962	Cammell Laird & Co. Ltd., Birkenhead
FIFE	D 20	1 June 1962			Fairfield Shipbuilding & Eng., Govan
GLAMORGAN	D 19	13 Sept. 1962			Vickers-Armstrongs, Newcastle-on-Tyne
HAMPSHIRE	D 06	24 Mar. 1959	16 Mar. 1961	15 Mar. 1963	John Brown & Co. Ltd., Clydebank
KENT	D 12	1 Mar. 1960	27 Sept. 1961	12 Aug. 1963	Harland & Wolff Ltd., Belfast
LONDON	D 16	26 Feb. 1960	7 Dec. 1961	22 Oct. 1963	Swan, Hunter & W. Richardson, Wallsend
NORFOLK	D 21	15 Mar. 1966	16 Nov. 1967		Swan, Hunter & W. Richardson, Wallsend

LONDON

TRUXTUN

To categorise this large, powerful and sophisticated fighting ship with the type of vessel known in other navies as frigates is plainly a misnomer. This latest so-called frigate or destroyer leader (a better term but still inadequate) is quite as big as a cruiser. Nuclear powered, and guided missile armed, she is clearly very formidable, and is fitted with every conceivable black box and gadget for combatant and operational efficiency including major equipment improvements, helicopter landing platform and hangar, bow mounted long range sonar, Navy tactical data system and three co-ordinate radar. But she is not as handsome as her predecessors as her two massive radar pylons detract from her symmetry.

A larger and improved nuclear powered guided missile "frigate", DLGN 36, was approved in the 1967 Fiscal Year new construction programme. Advance specifications called for: 10,150 tons full load displacement, 596 feet overall length, 61 feet beam, two dual "Tartar" SAM systems for AAW and ASW, one forward and one aft, two 5-inch gun mountings, one forward and one aft. Two more DLGNs were voted in the 1968 FY programme.

Standard displacement	Full load displacement	Length	Beam	Draught
8,200 tons	9,200 tons	564 feet	58 feet	31 feet
Guided weapons	*Guns*	*Torpedo Tubes*	*Anti-submarine weapons*	*Aircraft*
1 twin launcher for combined "Terrier"/"Asroc"	1–5 inch dual purpose 2–3 inch anti-aircraft	2–21 inch single 6–21 inch homing	ASROC (see guided weapons)	1 DAS helicopter

Propelling machinery	Shaft horse power	Nuclear reactors	Speed	Complement
Geared steam turbines	60,000	2 p.w.c. D 2 G	30 knots	479

Name	No.	Begun	Launched	Completed	Builders
TRUXTUN	DLGN 35	17 June 1963	19 Dec. 1964	27 May 1967	New York Shipbuilding Corp. N.J.

TRUXTUN

BAINBRIDGE

The world's first nuclear powered guided missile frigate, this remarkable prototype was built in the comparatively short time of less than $2\frac{1}{2}$ years. She was at once the largest warship of the destroyer type ever built (in the United States List of Naval Classifications she is placed under the generic destroyer category with the sub-classification of frigate) and the smallest surface warship to be nuclear powered. Her propulsion plant comprises two pressurised water cooled nuclear reactors generating steam for a two-shaft arrangement of geared turbines. The ship is capable of steaming 150,000 miles continuously at full power without refuelling, or 400,000 miles at 20 knots. The use of nuclear propulsion gives her many advantages. Among these are the tactical flexiblity of steaming at high speeds for long periods without the necessity for refuelling and the elimination of funnels and air intakes for fans, providing great protection for personnel against the danger of atomic fall-out. Also the elimination of smoke stacks permits the use of better radar and communication antennae located for optimum performance and free from the deteriorating effects of stack fumes. The ship has a flight apron on the quarter deck for helicopter land on and take off.

Standard displacement	Full load displacement	Length	Beam	Draught
7,600 tons	8,580 tons	564 feet	58 feet	29 feet

Guided weapons	Guns	Torpedo Tubes	Anti-submarine weapons	Aircraft
2 twin launchers for "Terrier" missiles	4–3 inch anti-aircraft (2 twin)	6–21 inch (2 triple)	1 octuple rocket launcher	1 helicopter

Propelling machinery	Shaft horse power	Nuclear reactors	Speed	Complement
Geared steam turbines	60,000	2 of p.w.c. D 1 G type	30 knots	450

Name	No.	Begun	Launched	Completed	Builders
BAINBRIDGE	DLGN 25	15 May 1959	15 Apr. 1961	6 Oct. 1962	Bethlehem Steel Company, Quincy

BAINBRIDGE

BELKNAP   FOX   JOSEPHUS DANIELS   STERETT   WILLIAM H. STANDLEY
BIDDLE   HORNE   JOUETT   WAINWRIGHT

A group of nine very large so-called frigates, or destroyer leaders, known as the "Belknap" class, these lithe looking ships with fine lines are as big as light cruisers. Their armament includes a twin ramp "Terrier" and "Asroc" dual launcher forward for surface-to-air guided missiles and anti-submarine rockets. They have a flight deck on the after shelter and are equipped with long range radar and sonar.

Standard displacement	Full load displacement	Length	Beam	Draught
6,570 tons	8,150 tons	547 feet	54¾ feet	28 feet
Guided weapons	Guns	Torpedo tubes	Anti-submarine	Aircraft
1 twin launcher for	1–5 inch dual purpose	2–21 inch single (removed)	ASROC	1 DAS helicopter
combined "Terrier"/ASROC	2–3 inch anti-aircraft	6–21 inch homing	(see guided weapons)	

Propelling machinery	Shaft horse power	Boilers	Speed	Complement
Geared steam turbines	85,000	4	34 knots	395

Name	No.	Begun	Launched	Completed	Builders
BELKNAP	DLG 26	5 Feb. 1962	20 July 1963	7 Nov. 1964	Bath Iron Works Corp.
BIDDLE	DLG 34	9 Dec. 1963	2 July 1965	21 Jan. 1967	Bath Iron Works Corp.
FOX	DLG 33	15 Jan. 1963	21 Nov. 1964	28 May 1966	Todd Shipyards Corp.
HORNE	DLG 30	12 Dec. 1962	30 Oct. 1964	15 Apr. 1967	San Francisco Naval Yard
JOSEPHUS DANIELS	DLG 27	23 Apr. 1962	2 Dec. 1963	8 May 1965	Bath Iron Works Corp.
JOUETT	DLG 29	25 Sept. 1962	30 June 1964	3 Dec. 1966	Puget Sound Naval Yard
STERETT	DLG 31	25 Sept. 1962	30 June 1964	8 Apr. 1967	Puget Sound Naval Yard
WAINWRIGHT	DLG 28	2 July 1962	25 Apr. 1964	8 Jan. 1966	Bath Iron Work Corp.
WILL. H. STANDLEY	DLG 32	29 July 1963	19 Dec. 1964	9 July 1966	Bath Iron Works Corp.

BIDDLE

DALE	GRIDLEY	HARRY E. YARNELL	REEVES	WORDEN
ENGLAND	HALSEY	LEAHY	RICHMOND L. TURNER	

Very large guided missile armed destroyer leaders or frigates approaching the light cruiser category. The design is an enlargement and improvement on that of the "Coontz" class, compared with which they mount guided weapons both forward and aft instead of aft only. Taking into consideration their novel superstructure and layout with combined mast-stacks or "macks" instead of the usual separate masts and stacks (funnels) they are quite symmetrical and good-looking vessels. They carry long range sonar and both long and short range anti-submarine weapons.

Standard displacement	Full load displacement	Length	Beam	Draught
5.670 tons	7.800 tons	533 feet	53½ feet	24½ feet

Guided weapons	Guns	Torpedo tubes	Anti-submarine weapons
2 twin launchers for "Terrier" missiles	4–3 inch anti-aircraft (2 twin)	6–21 inch (3 twin)	1 octuple rocket launcher (ASROC)

Propelling machinery	Shaft horse power	Boilers	Speed	Complement
Geared steam turbines	85,000	4	34 knots	372

Name	No.	Begun	Launched	Completed	Builders
DALE	DLG 19	6 Sept. 1960	28 July 1962	2 Nov. 1963	New York S.B. Corp.
ENGLAND	DLG 22	4 Oct. 1960	6 Mar. 1962	7 Dec. 1963	Todd Shipyards Corp.
GRIDLEY	DLG 21	15 July 1960	31 July 1961	25 May 1963	Puget Sound B. & D. Co.
HALSEY	DLG 23	26 Aug. 1960	15 Jan. 1962	20 July 1963	San Francisco N.S.Y.
HARRY E. YARNELL	DLG 17	31 May 1960	9 Dec. 1961	2 Feb. 1963	Bath Iron Works Corp.
LEAHY	DLG 16	3 Dec 1959	1 July 1961	4 Aug. 1962	Bath Iron Works Corp.
REEVES	DLG 24	1 July 1960	12 May 1962	16 May 1964	Puget Sound N.S.Y.
RICHMOND K. TURNER	DLG 20	9 Jan. 1961	6 Apr. 1963	28 May 1964	New York S.B. Corp.
WORDEN	DLG 18	19 Sept. 1960	2 June 1962	3 Aug. 1963	Bath Iron Works Corp.

DALE

COONTZ	DEWEY	KING	MACDONOUGH	PREBLE
DAHLGREN	FARRAGUT	LUCE	MAHAN	WILLIAM V. PRATT

Guided-missile ships of the destroyer leader or large frigate category, these ten vessels are improved versions of the original destroyer leaders of the "Mitscher" type, afterwards re-rated as frigates. Designed to destroy air targets, these new ships of the "Coontz" class also have anti-submarine and airborne early-warning capabilities. They have a conventional battery forward and a twin "Terrier" guided-missile launcher aft.

Standard displacement	*Full load displacement*	*Length*	*Beam*	*Draught*
4,700 tons	5,800 tons	512½ feet	52⅓ feet	25 feet

Guided weapons	*Main guns*	*Anti-aircraft guns*	*Torpedo tubes*	*Anti-submarine weapons*
1 twin launcher for "Terrier" missiles	1–5 inch dual purpose	4–3 inch (2 twin)	6–21 inch fixed (2 triple)	ASROC 8-tube "Pepperbox" launcher

Propelling machinery	*Shaft horse power*	*Boilers*	*Speed*	*Complement*
Geared steam turbines	85,000	4	34 knots	359

Name	*No.*	*Begun*	*Launched*	*Completed*	*Builders*
COONTZ	DLG 9	2 Mar. 1957	6 Dec. 1958	15 July 1960	Puget Sound Naval Shipyard
DAHLGREN	DLG 12	1 Mar. 1958	16 Mar. 1960	15 July 1961	Philadelphia Naval Shipyard
DEWEY	DLG 14	10 Aug. 1957	30 Nov. 1958	7 Dec. 1959	Bath Iron Works, Bath, Maine
FARRAGUT	DLG 6	3 June 1957	18 July 1958	17 Feb. 1961	Bethlehem Steel Co., Quincy
KING	DLG 10	2 Mar. 1957	6 Dec. 1958	17 Nov. 1960	Puget Sound Naval Shipyard
LUCE	DLG 7	1 Oct. 1957	11 Dec. 1958	15 July 1961	Bethlehem Steel Co., Quincy
MACDONOUGH	DLG 8	15 Apr. 1958	9 July 1959	12 Jan. 1962	Bethlehem Steel Co., Quincy
MAHAN	DLG 11	29 July 1957	7 Oct. 1959	28 Nov. 1960	San Francisco Naval Shipyard
PREBLE	DLG 15	16 Dec. 1957	23 May 1959	9 May 1960	Bath Iron Works, Bath, Maine
WILLIAM V. PRATT	DLG 13	1 Mar. 1958	16 Mar. 1960	30 Dec. 1961	Philadelphia Naval Shipyard

MACDONOUGH

MITSCHER   JOHN S. McCAIN   WILLIS A. LEE   WILKINSON

These ships of the "Mitscher" class were projected and laid down as destroyers, and were in fact the largest destroyers ever built in the United States and in the world, being larger than ships formerly rated as light cruisers in other countries. Of a new design specifically constructed as a long-range fleet type for both administrative and anti-submarine duties, they carried modern surface, underwater and anti-aircraft weapons, and were equipped with newly developed electronic devices for hunter-killer missions. Their 5-inch guns are fully automatic loading, rapid firing and radar controlled. Newer longer range 3-inch, 70-calibre mountings were installed in 1957–8 in place of their former 3-inch, 50-calibre guns, and their four 20-mm. anti-aircraft guns were removed. The after twin 3-inch mountings were subsequently removed to provide a helicopter platform. The propelling machinery, of light weight, included many advanced engineering features not previously installed in fighting ships. *Mitscher* and *John S. McCain* have different propulsion plants from those in *Willis A. Lee* and *Wilkinson*. All four were re-rated as destroyer leaders while still under construction in 1951, but were again re-classified as frigates early in 1955. *Mitscher* and *John S. McCain* were converted into guided missile destroyers in 1966–68.

Standard displacement	Full load displacement	Length	Beam	Draught
3,675 tons	4,730 tons	493 feet	50 feet	26 feet

Guided weapons	Main guns	Anti-aircraft guns	Anti-submarine weapons	Aircraft
1 single launcher for "Tartar" missiles (DDG)	2–5 inch dual purpose (DL) 1–5 inch dual purpose (DDG)	2–3 inch (twin) (DL)	1 ASROC 8-tube launcher (DDG) 2 triple torpedo launchers (DL, DDG)	1 helicopter (DL) 2 DASH (DDG)

Propelling machinery	Shaft horse power	Boilers	Speed	Complement
Geared steam turbines	80,000	4CE (DDG), 4 FW (DL)	35 knots	339

Name	No.	Begun	Launched	Completed	Builders
MITSCHER	DDG 35 (ex-DL2, ex-DD 927)	3 Oct. 1949	26 Jan. 1952	16 May 1953	Bath Iron Works
JOHN S. MCCAIN	DDG 36 (ex-DL3, ex-DD 928)	24 Oct. 1949	12 July 1952	12 Oct. 1953	Bath Iron Works
WILLIS A. LEE	DL 4 (ex-DD 929)	1 Nov. 1949	26 Jan. 1952	28 Sept. 1954	Bethlehem Steel Co.
WILKINSON	DL 5 (ex-DD 930)	1 Feb. 1950	22 Apr. 1952	29 July 1954	Bethlehem Steel Co.

WILKINSON

NORFOLK

A rather peculiar vessel of hybrid type, difficult to classify, this ship was first designated a cruiser, hunter-killer ship, subsequently re-classified as a destroyer leader, and again re-classified as a frigate early in 1955. On a cruiser hull she mounted the armament of a destroyer, and was intended as a flagship for destroyers accompanying a heavy task force, her heavier displacement enabling her to carry the accumulation of modern anti-submarine and anti-aircraft devices impossible to mount in a destroyer hull. Her design was evolved in the light of nuclear experiments, and it was hoped and believed in the American Navy that neither atomic explosions nor weather would hinder this remarkable ship from operating at her full efficiency at all times. She was fitted with newly-developed communications equipment, including radar, sonar and electronics gear. Her former eight 20-mm. anti-aircraft guns were removed. In general appearance she has a bow view similar to that of "Mitscher" class destroyer leaders or frigates, see previous page, although she is a considerably larger ship.

Standard displacement	Full load displacement	Length	Beam	Draught
5,600 tons	7,300 tons	540¼ feet	54¼ feet	26 feet

Main and Anti-aircraft guns	Torpedo tubes	Anti-submarine weapons	
8–3 inch dual purpose	2 triple launchers	1 ASROC 8-tube launcher, 2–12.75 Alfa rocket launchers	

Propelling machinery	Shaft horse power	Boilers	Speed	Complement
Geared steam turbines	80,000	4 Babcock & Wilcox	32 knots	411

Name	No.	Begun	Launched	Completed	Builders
NORFOLK	DL 1 (ex-CLK 1)	1 Sept. 1949	29 Dec. 1951	4 Mar. 1953	New York Shipbuilding Corp.

NORFOLK

5 "KRESTA" CLASS

These are a new type of guided missile armed destroyers known as the "Kresta" class (NATO designation) and commissioned for operational service from early 1967 onwards. In construction they appear to be hybrid or dual-purpose anti-submarine warfare and guided missile armed major warships of the broad super-destroyer or light cruiser-frigate type. The design seems to be a combination of that of the immediately preceding and successive "Kashin" and "Kynda" classes of powerful destroyers and a logical follow-on from the recently built "Kashin" class, but of slightly enlarged and more sophisticated type and provided with a helicopter hangar and flight apron. The prototype ship was laid down in September 1964, launched in 1965 and completed sufficiently for sea trials in February 1967, quite a considerable building achievement for a fighting vessel of her size, power and complexity. She was built at the Zhdanov Shipyard, Leningrad, where four sister ships followed her off the stocks in quick succession, and carried out first proving tests in the Baltic.

It is interesting to compare the layout and appearance of this class with the general arrangement and armament disposition of the preceding "Kashin", "Kynda", "Krupny" and "Kildin" classes, see photographs on following pages.

Standard displacement	Full load displacement	Length	Beam	Draught
6,000 tons	7,000 tons	$508\frac{1}{2}$ feet	$55\frac{3}{4}$ feet	20 feet

Guided weapons	Guns	Anti-submarine armament	Torpedo tubes	Aircraft
2 twin launchers for s-to-s	4–57 mm. A.A.	2 12-barrel launchers	10–21 inch	2 helicopters
2 twin launchers for s-to-a	(2 twin)	2 6-barrel launchers	(2 quintuple)	

Propelling machinery	Shaft horse power	Speed	Complement
4 gas turbines	100,000	36 knots	440

"KRESTA" Class

ADMIRAL GOLOVKO	GROM	GROZNY	VARYAG

This class of guided missile armed ships, known as the "Kynda" class by NATO designation, represent a novel type of large destroyers akin to light cruisers, and in addition to being very formidably armed with all kinds of modern weapons have all the appearance of both offensive and defensive cruisers. They appear to be something more than a natural development of the earlier types of Soviet destroyers fitted with guided weapons. Building to this new design is believed to have commenced in 1960 with the first vessel of the class laid down in June: she was launched in April 1961 at the Zhdanov Shipyard, Leningrad, and completed in June 1962. Their appearance is very distinctive with two enclosed towers instead of masts stepped forward of each rake funnel. They are starkly handsome ships and quite symmetrical. They have a helicopter spot landing apron on the stern. They are highly manoeuvrable with two screws and two rudders. The ships are officially known in the Soviet Union, and popularly referred to by other countries, as rocket cruisers. There are believed to be four ships, although numbers painted on their hulls from time to time, probably changed according to assignment and geographical location, are 202, 239, 299, 343, 641 and 898, but only four names have been recorded.

Standard displacement	Full load displacement	Length	Beam	Draught
4,800 tons	6,000 tons	492 feet	51 feet	19 feet

Guided weapons	Guns	Anti-submarine armament	Torpedo tubes	Aircraft
2 quadruple launchers for s-to-s 1 twin launcher for s-to-a	4–3.3 inch (2 twin)	2 12-barrel launchers	6-21 inch (2 triple)	Helicopter

Propelling machinery	Shaft horse power	Boilers	Speed	Complement
2 sets Cosag turbines	85,000	4	35 knots	400

"KYNDA" class

DUQUESNE   SUFFREN

Suffren was the prototype of a new class of French guided missile armed ships ordered in the 1960 new construction programme. She was originally designed as a guided missile cruiser and officially known as such on the project schedule until 1961, but as she more nearly approximated to the current American destroyer leader/frigate category she was reclassified as a guided missile frigate in conformity with United States Navy practice. The structure of the ship provides the best possible resistance to atomic blast. She is fitted with up-to-date detection devices, two sonars and tactical information system. Carefully studied habitability is a feature of the design, and she is equipped with stabilisers. She was originally to have carried an anti-submarine helicopter. There are only two ships of the class instead of the three initially projected, although other frigates of the same type but of larger size are envisaged. There were several recastings of the design before the present somewhat bizarre "ham and onion" mast/funnel and domed superstructure was finalised.

Standard displacement	Full load displacement	Length	Beam	Draught
5,100 tons	6,000 tons	518 feet	51 feet	20 feet
Guided weapons	Guns	Anti-submarine		Torpedo launchers
1 twin launcher for	2–3.9 inch A.A.	1 launcher for		4 (2 each side)
"Masurca" missiles	2–30 mm. A.A.	"Malafon" rockets		for A/S homing

Propelling machinery	Shaft horse power	Boilers	Speed	Complement
Geared steam turbines	72,500	4 automatic	34 knots	426

Name	No.	Begun	Launched	Trials	Operational	Builders
DUQUESNE	D 603	12 Nov. 1964	12 Feb. 1966	July 1968	1969	Brest Naval Dockyard
SUFFREN	D 602	21 Dec. 1962	15 May 1965	Dec. 1965	1968	Lorient Naval Dockyard

SUFFREN

ANDREA DORIA
CAIO DUILIO

Of considerable interest to naval architects, these new escort cruisers or destroyer leaders of an entirely novel design specifically projected to carry both guided-missile launchers and heavy anti-submarine helicopters, are extraordinarily beamy in relation to their length. The "Terrier" surface-to-air guided-missile battery is operated from a twin mounting forward. The helicopters operate from a large flight deck or hover apron aft, a platform measuring $98\frac{1}{2}$ by $52\frac{1}{2}$ feet. The anti-aircraft battery includes eight 3-inch fully automatic guns of a new pattern, disposed in single turrets, four on each side amidships abreast the funnels and the bridge. They have a rate of fire of 70 rounds per minute. These very unusual ships are officially rated as *Incrociatori di Scorta*. They perpetuate the names of battleships scrapped. They approximate to the United States guided-missile frigate or destroyer leader category, DLG.

Standard displacement	Full load displacement	Length	Beam	Draught
5,300 tons	6,500 tons	$489\frac{3}{4}$ feet	$56\frac{1}{2}$ feet	$16\frac{1}{4}$ feet

Anti-aircraft guns	Guided weapons	Torpedo tubes	Aircraft
8–3 inch (single)	1 twin launcher for "Terrier" missiles	6–12 inch A/S (2 triple)	4 A/B 240 B ASW helicopters

Propelling machinery	Shaft horse power	Boilers	Speed	Complement
Geared steam turbines	60,000	4 Foster-Wheeler	31 knots	478

Name	No.	Begun	Launched	Completed	Builders
ANDREA DORIA	553	11 May 1958	17 Feb. 1963	23 Feb. 1964	Cantieri del Tirreno, Riva Trigoso
CAIO DUILIO	554	16 May 1958	22 Dec. 1962	30 Nov. 1964	Navalmeccanica, Castellammare di Stabia

ANDREA DORIA

SAN GIORGIO   SAN MARCO

These vessels have had a chequered career. They were originally built as *Pompeo Magno* and *Giulio Germanico*, respectively of the *"Capitani Romani"* (Roman Captains) class, and rated first as *Exploratori Oceanici* (Ocean Scouts) and then as light cruisers. *Giulio Germanico* was sunk by the Germans in Sept. 1943 before completion, but refloated in 1947. Both ships were converted into fleet destroyers by Cantieri del Tirreno, Genova, and Navalmeccanica Castellammare di Stabia, respectively, being completed in the autumn of 1955 and recommissioned on 1 July 1955 and 20 Feb. 1956. They were re-rated as *Exploratori* (scouts) in 1957 and as *Cacciatorpediniere Conduttori* (destroyer leaders) in 1958. *San Georgio* was reconstructed, re-engined and rearmed as a training ship at the Naval Dockyard, La Spezia, in 1963–65.

	Standard displacement	Full load displacement	Length	Beam	Draught
San Marco:	4,000 tons	5,260 tons	466¼ feet	47¼ feet	21 feet
San Giorgio:	3,950 tons	4,450 tons			

	Main guns	Anti-aircraft guns	Anti-submarine weapons	Complement
San Marco:	6–5 inch	20–40 mm.	3-barrelled depth charge mortar (both)	484
San Giorgio:	4–5 inch	3–3 inch	6–12 inch torpedo tubes (S.G. only)	348 + 130 cadets

	Propelling machinery	Shaft horse power	Boilers	Speed
San Marco:	Geared steam turbines	110,000	4 of 3-drum type (S.M. only)	38 knots
San Giorgio:	Gas turbines and diesels	15,000 and 16,600		28 knots

Name	No.	Begun	Launched	Completed	Builders
SAN GIORGIO	D 562	23 Sept. 1939	28 Aug. 1941	24 June 1943	C. N. Riuniti, Ancona
SAN MARCO	D 563	11 May 1940	20 July 1941	19 Jan. 1956	Navalmeccanica Castellammare di Stabia

Note: Two sister ships, the former Italian light cruisers *Attilio Regolo* and *Scipione Africano*, allocated to France in 1948 as her share of surrendered Italian ships, and renamed *Chateaurenault* and *Guichen*, respectively, were stricken from the list in 1962.

SAN GIORGIO

DESTROYERS

THE word destroyer was a diminutive of the older term "torpedo-boat destroyer", self-explanatory of the vessel's original function. In 1892 the menace of torpedo-boats was so formidable that it was resolved to take special measures against them. The result was the construction of torpedo-boat destroyers. In designing the first destroyers the evolution of a decade was bridged by taking the characteristics of torpedo-boats and expanding them to twice the displacement of the craft they were intended to destroy. The first British destroyers, *Havock* and *Hornet*, displaced 240 tons and carried a 12-pounder gun, three 6-pounders and one 18-inch torpedo tube, reciprocating engines giving them a speed of 26½ knots. The success of these ships, which proved to be good sea-boats, justified the construction of destroyers on a large scale. The first destroyers propelled by turbines were *Viper* and *Cobra* of 400 tons, designed for a speed of 35 knots. In a decade the torpedo-boat destroyer had usurped the functions of the torpedo-boat itself which was rendered ineffective and obsolete. The two types had practically merged. By 1906–8 British destroyers had grown progressively through the A, B, C, D, and E classes into the F class of ocean-going ships of 855 to 1,062 tons with two 4-inch guns and two 18-inch torpedo tubes, oil-fired boilers and turbines giving speeds of 35 knots. With the passing of the 1,000 ton displacement mark, the adoption of oil fuel and the introduction of the 4-inch gun the shape of the modern destroyer could be discerned. The last coal-fired British destroyers were the "G" class, 1910, in which 21-inch torpedoes were introduced. By the outbreak of the First World War in 1914 some 240 destroyers had been built. Developed through the H, I, K, L, M, N, O and P boats, about 280 destroyers were built during the period of hostilities. Geared turbines instead of direct turbines were installed, resulting in an increase of speed to 36 knots, and the R, S, T and U group were of basically standard design to which the bulk of the destroyers were built during the war, and a dozen were still in service in 1939, eight surviving until the end of the Second World War. In the V and W boats a great advance in fighting power was effected, and the design of these ships remained the essential pattern upon which were based all subsequent destroyers built between the two great wars, not only in Great Britain but all over the world. No fewer than 54 of the V and W class were still in service in 1939 and over 40 survived until 1946 after careers of over a quarter of a century. By the end of the First World War the destroyers' original function of destroying torpedo-boats was almost completely extraneous to its many and varied new duties. Although the main use of destroyers was with the battle fleet, to ward off enemy destroyers and torpedo-attack the enemy battle fleet, it was as anti-submarine hunters and killers that they shone. During the 1914–18 war Britain lost 69 destroyers. Of the 370 which survived the war many were soon scrapped. In 1922 there were only 185 left, a number which remained fairly constant between the wars by scrapping old ones as new vessels were built. No new destroyers were laid down for ten years after the Armistice except the experimental *Ambuscade* and *Amazon*. Then a new alphabetical cycle was initiated, the 68 destroyers of the "A" to "I" flotillas, completed 1930–8, displacing 1,335 to 1,375 tons with four 4.7-inch guns, eight 21-inch torpedo tubes, and speeds of 35–36 knots. There followed the large "Tribal" class of 16 units, completed in 1938–9, displacing 1,870 tons, heavily armed with eight 4.7-inch guns in twin shields, seven smaller guns and four 21-inch tubes, and steaming at 36½ knots. The 24 vessels of the J, K and N flotillas of 1,760 tons mounted six 4.7-inch guns, six smaller weapons and ten 21-inch torpedo tubes, and the 16 of the L and M flotillas completed early in the Second World War displaced 1,920 tons. The alphabetical cycle was completed during the war with O, P, Q, R, S, T, U, V, W, and Z flotillas, followed by the "C", "Battle", "Weapon" and "Daring" classes, see following pages. In 1939 Britain had 180 destroyers. During the war 140 were lost; some 220 were built and 50 were acquired from the United States. About 280 were listed in 1946. In 1955 Britain had 80 destroyers and in 1969 she had 20. The United States has 340 destroyers, 33 destroyer leaders, and 250 destroyer escorts. The Soviet Union has 120 destroyers.

DAINTY   DECOY   DEFENDER   DIAMOND   DIANA   DUCHESS

The largest orthodox destroyers in the Royal Navy, the eight units of the "Daring" class represented a development and a combination of the "Battle" and "Weapon" designs. Basically a wartime conception they embodied the latest ideas in warship construction and incorporated many features new to British ships. Their propelling machinery used higher steam pressures and temperatures than ever before. Their after bank of quintuple torpedo tubes was removed in 1958. *Daring* and *Delight* were put on the disposal list in 1968. Three more destroyers of the "Daring" class, the *Vampire*, *Vendetta* and *Voyager*, were built in Australia for the Royal Australian Navy. *Voyager* sank after collision with the aircraft carrier *Melbourne* on 10 Feb. 1964 and was replaced by *Duchess*, lent from the Royal Navy.

Standard displacement	Full load displacement	Length	Beam	Draught
2,810 tons	3,600 tons	388½ feet	43 feet	18 feet

Main guns	Anti-aircraft guns	Torpedo tubes	Anti-submarine weapons	Complement
6–4.5 inch	2 or 6–40 mm.	5–21 inch	"Squid" triple barrelled depth charge mortar	297

Propelling machinery	Shaft horse power	Boilers	Speed
Geared steam turbines	54,000	2 Foster Wheeler or 2 Babcock & Wilcox	34.75 knots

Name	No.	Begun	Launched	Completed	Builders
DAINTY	D 108	17 Dec. 1945	16 Aug. 1950	26 Feb. 1953	J. Samuel White & Co. Ltd., Cowes
DECOY	D 106	22 Sept. 1946	29 Mar. 1949	28 Apr. 1953	Yarrow & Co. Ltd., Scotstoun, Glasgow
DEFENDER	D 114	22 Mar. 1949	27 July 1950	5 Dec. 1952	Alex. Stephen & Sons Ltd., Govan
DIAMOND	D 35	15 Mar. 1949	14 June 1950	21 Feb. 1952	John Brown & Co. Ltd., Clydebank
DIANA	D 126	3 Apr. 1947	8 May 1952	29 Mar. 1954	Yarrow & Co. Ltd., Scotstoun, Glasgow
DUCHESS	D 154	2 July 1948	9 Apr. 1951	23 Oct. 1952	John I. Thornycroft & Co. Ltd., Woolston

Note: Of the four destroyers of the "Weapon" class, converted into radar pickets, *Battleaxe* was scrapped in 1964 and *Scorpion* in 1966, *Broadsword* was listed for scrap in 1967, and *Crossbow* was relegated to harbour training ship in 1967.

DIAMOND

AGINCOURT	AISNE	BARROSA	CORUNNA

These four ships are the survivors of the Later "Battle" class destroyers. In 1961–62 they were completely reconstructed and converted into Fleet Radar Pickets, or aircraft direction destroyers. Little remained of the original ships except the hull, engines and boilers. Internally they were entirely redesigned to give a higher standard of fighting efficiency and habitability. The operations room was one of the most complex and compact ever contrived in destroyers. The fifth 4·5-inch gun abaft the funnel, the eight 40-mm. anti-aircraft guns in four twin mountings, and the ten 21-inch torpedo tubes in two quintuple banks of the original ships were suppressed. A beam to beam lattice foremast was stepped across the ship to support the massive "double bedstead" radar, and the "Seacat" guided missile launcher was mounted on the after end of the superstructure.

Standard displacement	Full load displacement	Length	Beam	Draught
2,780 tons	3,430 tons	379 feet	40½ feet	17½ feet

Main guns	Guided weapons	Anti-submarine weapons	Complement
4–4.5 inch (2 twin)	1 quadruple launcher for "Seacat" missiles	"Squid" triple barrelled depth charge mortar	268

Propelling machinery	Shaft horse power	Boilers	Speed
Geared steam turbines	50,000	2 Admiralty 3-drum type	35.75 knots

Name	No.	Begun	Launched	Completed	Builders
AGINCOURT	D 86	12 Dec. 1943	29 June 1945	25 June 1947	Hawthorn Leslie & Co. Ltd., Hebburn-on-Tyne
AISNE	D 22	26 Aug. 1943	12 May 1945	20 Mar. 1947	Vickers-Armstrongs Ltd., Newcastle-on-Tyne
BARROSA	D 68	28 Dec. 1943	17 Jan. 1945	14 Feb. 1947	John Brown & Co. Ltd., Clydebank
CORUNNA	D 97	12 Apr. 1944	29 May 1945	6 June 1947	Swan, Hunter & Wig. Richardson, Wallsend

Note: Of the four unconverted units of the Later "Battle" class, *Alamein, Dunkirk* and *Jutland* were scrapped in 1965 and *Matapan*, in reserve, was scheduled to be converted into a trials ship in 1969.

Of the sixteen destroyers of the Early "Battle" class, *Cadiz* and *Gabbard* were sold to Pakistan in 1956 and renamed *Khaibar* and *Badr*, respectively; *Hogue* was discarded for scrap in 1960, *Gravelines, St. James* and *St. Kitts* in 1961, *Vigo* was scrapped in 1964, *Armada, Barfleur* and *Finisterre* in 1965, followed by *Camperdown, Lagos, Solebay* and *Trafalgar. Sluys* was sold to Iran in 1967. *Saintes* became tender to *Caledonia* training establishment before disposal.

Two Australian-built "Battle" class destroyers are in the Royal Australian Navy, *Anzac* as training ship, *Tobruk* in reserve

BARROSA

CAMBRIAN   CAPRICE   CARYSFORT   CAVALIER

Originally there were four flotillas of eight ships, the "Ca", "Ch", "Co" and "Cr" classes. *Crescent* and *Crusader* were transferred to the Royal Canadian Navy. *Charity*, *Chivalrous*, *Creole* and *Crispin* were sold to the Royal Pakistan Navy and renamed *Shah Jahan*, *Taimur*, *Alamgir* and *Jahangir* respectively, and *Cromwell*, *Crown*, *Crystal* and *Croziers* were sold to the Royal Norwegian Navy as *Bergen*, *Oslo*, *Stavanger* and *Trondheim* respectively. Originally all ships had four 4.5-inch guns, but there were subsequently many variations. They were latterly reconstructed, modernised and converted for anti-submarine warfare, and standardised to two types, one with three 4.5-inch guns, the other with two 4.5-inch guns and fitted for minelaying. *Carysfort* and *Cavalier* have different bridges from *Cambrian* and *Caprice* which have frigate type bridges.

Standard displacement	Full load displacement	Length	Beam	Draught
2,106 tons	2,749 tons	362¾ feet	35⅔ feet	17 feet

Main guns	Anti-aircraft guns	Torpedo tubes	Anti-submarine weapons	
3–4.5 inch	4–40 mm.	4–21 inch	2 "Squid" triple barrelled depth charge mortars	

Propelling machinery	Shaft horse power	Boilers	Speed	Complement
Parsons geared turbines	40,000	2 Admiralty 3-drum type	36.75 knots	186

Name	No.	Begun	Launched	Completed	Builders
CAMBRIAN	D 85	14 Aug. 1942	10 Dec. 1943	17 July 1944	Scott's S.B. & Eng. Co. Ltd., Greenock
CAPRICE	D 01	28 Sept. 1942	16 Sept. 1943	5 Apr. 1944	Yarrow & Co. Ltd., Scotstoun, Glasgow
CARYSFORT	D 25	12 May 1943	25 July 1944	20 Feb. 1945	J. Samuel White & Co. Ltd., Cowes, I. of W.
CAVALIER	D 73	28 Feb. 1943	7 Apr. 1944	22 Nov. 1944	J. Samuel White & Co. Ltd., Cowes, I. of W.

Note: Of the "Ch" and "Co" classes, *Constance* was scrapped in 1956, *Comus* in 1958, *Contest* and *Cossack* in 1960. *Cheviot,* *Chieftain*, *Childers*, *Cockade*, *Comet*, *Concord* and *Consort* in 1962, and *Chaplet*, *Chequers* and *Chevron* in 1963.

Of the "Ca" class, *Caesar*, *Carron* (disarmed as navigation tender in 1960 and discarded in 1963), *Cassandra* and *Cavendish* were scrapped in 1967.

CAMBRIAN

BARNEY	**BUCHANAN**	**HENRY B. WILSON**	**LYNDE McCORMICK**	**SEMMES**
BENJAMIN	**CHARLES F. ADAMS**	**HOEL**	**RICHARD E. BYRD**	**TATTNALL**
STODDERT	**COCHRANE**	**JOHN KING**	**ROBISON**	**TOWERS**
BERKELEY	**CONYNGHAM**	**JOSEPH STRAUSS**	**SAMPSON**	**WADDELL**
BIDDLE	**GOLDSBOROUGH**	**LAWRENCE**	**SELLERS**	

Guided-missile armed ships of the destroyer category, these vessels of the "Charles F. Adams" class are equipped to launch "Tartar" surface-to-air missiles which are smaller than "Terrier" weapons with greater range. They are also armed with two main singly-mounted rapid-firing 5-inch guns and the latest anti-submarine weapons. As compared with previous destroyers the new ships have greater overall length, a wider beam and heavier displacement. They have a new hull design which is an evolution of that of the "Forrest Sherman" class destroyers and like the latter have aluminium superstructures. The most recent habitability improvements were incorporated into their construction, including the air conditioning of all living spaces. The 23 ships were laid down in 1958–62 and launched in 1959–63 for completion in 1960–64. The original design provided for two 5-inch guns, one forward in "A" position and one aft in "Y" position, with anti-submarine weapons in "B" position and guided missiles in "X" position, but the after 5-inch gun in "Y" position was transposed in favour of a guided-missile launcher. 42 missiles are carried .They have a range of 15 to 20 miles. Three more guided missile destroyers of this class were built for Australia and three for West Germany.

Standard displacement	Full load displacement	Length	Beam	Draught
3,370 tons	4,500 tons	432 feet	47 feet	20 feet

Main guns	Guided weapons	Anti-submarine weapons	Complement
2–5 inch dual purpose	1 twin or single launcher for "Tartar" missiles	1 ASROC 8-tube launcher	354

Propelling machinery	Shaft horse power	Boilers	Speed
Geared steam turbines	70,000	4	35 knots

JOSEPH STRAUSS

DESTROYERS (DDG & DD)   *United States of America*

DECATUR ⎫
JOHN PAUL JONES ⎪ DDG
PARSONS ⎪
SOMERS ⎭

BARRY
BIGELOW
BLANDY
DAVIS
DU PONT

EDSON
FORREST SHERMAN
HULL
JONAS INGRAM
MANLEY

MORTON
MULLINIX
RICHARD S. EDWARDS
TURNER JOY

As built the largest conventionally armed American destroyers, these vessels of the "Forrest Sherman" class were not radical in design, but embodied certain improvements in armament. They had increased freeboard aft, and the entire ship's structure above the main deck, including gun foundations, was of aluminium to obtain the maximum stability while maintaining the minimum displacement. They were air conditioned throughout. The 5-inch dual purpose guns in single turret mountings were originally disposed one forward and two aft. The 3-inch anti-aircraft guns were in new pattern twin enclosed gunhouses. Tubes were replaced by torpedo racks between the funnels. *Barry* was fitted with a new clipper bow housing a new type of sonar dome and has stem anchor only. *Decatur, John Paul Jones, Parsons* and *Somers* were converted into guided missile destroyers (DDG) in 1965–68.

Standard displacement	Full load displacement	Length	Beam	Draught
2,850 tons	4,050 tons	418½ feet	45 feet	20 feet

Guided weapons	Main guns	Anti-aircraft guns	Anti-submarine weapons
1 single launcher for "Tartar" missiles (DDG)	2–5 inch dual purpose (DD) 1–5 inch dual purpose (DDG)	2–3 inch (DD)	1 ASROC 8-tube launcher 2 triple torpedo launchers

Propelling machinery	Shaft horse power	Boilers	Speed	Complement
Geared steam turbines	70,000	4	33 knots	276 to 337

All eighteen ships were laid down in 1953–7, launched in 1955–8 and completed in 1955–9, the *Forrest Sherman* being the first and name-ship of the class. Builders: Bath Iron Works Corp., Bath, Maine: *Forrest Sherman, John Paul Jones, Barry, Manley, Du Pont, Bigelow, Hull, Edson* and *Somers*. Bethlehem Steel Co., Quincy: *Decatur, Davis, Jonas Ingram, Blandy* and *Mullinix*. Ingalls Shipbuilding Corp.: *Morton* and *Parsons*. Puget Sound Bridge & Dredging Co., Seattle: *Richard S. Edwards* and *Turner Joy*.

SOMERS

G

CARPENTER	HARWOOD	LLOYD THOMAS	NORRIS
FRED T. BERRY	KEPPLER	McCAFFERY	ROBERT A. OWENS

Originally intended as units of the "Gearing" class fleet destroyers, these ships were converted to form a fast, long-range anti-submarine striking force. Additional multiple anti-submarine mortars were installed amidships and aft, and a number of sono-buoys were included in the equipment. These were dropped in a diamond-shaped pattern (one in the middle) outlining an area in which a submarine was suspected to be in operation. They contained microphones, and by keeping track of which picked up the loudest sound the destroyer could determine in which direction and at what speed and depth the submarine was moving. Once this was detected the destroyer moved in rapidly for the kill, laying down a pattern of depth bombs. These ships were classified as DDE (i.e. fleet destroyers [DD] modified for escort duties [E]), but they were originally described as DDK, hunter-killer destroyers. Redesignated DD in 1963. The first line in the tabulated details refers to *Carpenter* and *Robert A. Owens* only.

	Standard displacement	*Full load displacement*	*Length*	*Beam*	*Draught*
C. & R.A.O.:	2,425 tons	3,410 tons	$390\frac{1}{2}$ feet	41 feet	19 feet
Others:	2,425 tons	3,500 tons			

Main guns	*Torpedo tubes*	*Anti-submarine weapons*
2–5 inch	2–21 inch	1 ASROC 8-tube launcher, 2 triple torpedo launchers, DASH facilities
4–5 inch		2 triple torpedo launchers, 2 drone anti-submarine helicopters (DASH)

Propelling machinery	*Shaft horse power*	*Boilers*	*Speed*	*Complement*
Geared steam turbines	60,000	4	34 knots	264 to 291

All eight ships were launched in 1945–6. *Robert A. Owens* was built by Bath Iron Works Corp.; *Keppler* and *Lloyd Thomas* by Bethlehem, San Francisco; *Fred T. Berry*, *Harwood*, *McCaffery* and *Norris* by Bethlehem, San Pedro; and *Carpenter* by Consolidated Steel Corp. (completed by Newport News).

KEPPLER

| BASILONE | EPPERSON | NEW | ROBERT L. WILSON |
| DAMATO | HOLDER | RICH | |

These seven vessels were further conversions of the "Gearing" class destroyers, somewhat similar to the "Carpenter" class previously described. The *Basilone* and *Epperson* had for a long time been suspended and laid up in an incomplete state after the Second World War, but they were eventually resumed and converted for anti-submarine warfare, and were completed as escort destroyers. They were armed with new weapons and were equipped with improved sonar and other electronic gear. The other five units were converted into escort destroyers after having been in service as fleet destroyers and they were also redesignated from DD to DDE. All were redesignated DD in 1963. The 3-inch anti-aircraft batteries and the conventional torpedo tube mountings were removed.

Standard displacement	Full load displacement	Length	Beam	Draught
2,425 tons	3,500 tons	390½ feet	41 feet	19 feet

Main guns	Anti-submarine weapons
4–5 inch	1 ASROC 8-tube launcher, 2 triple torpedo launchers, 2 drone anti-submarine helicopters

Propelling machinery	Shaft horse power	Boilers	Speed	Complement
Geared steam turbines	60,000	4	34 knots	264 to 274

Name	Launched	Completed	Builders
BASILONE	21 Dec. 1945	21 July 1949	Consolidated Steel Corp.
DAMATO	21 Nov. 1945	26 Apr. 1946	Bethlehem, Staten Island
EPPERSON	22 Dec. 1945	19 Mar. 1949	Federal S. B. & D. D. Co.
HOLDER	25 Aug. 1945	17 May 1946	Consolidated Steel Corp.
NEW	18 Aug. 1945	4 Apr. 1946	Consolidated Steel Corp.
RICH	5 Oct. 1945	2 July 1946	Consolidated Steel Corp.
ROBERT L. WILSON	5 Jan. 1946	28 Mar. 1946	Bath Iron Works Corp.

EPPERSON

AGERHOLM	GEORGE H. McKENZIE	LEONARD F. MASON	SAMUEL B. ROBERTS
ARNOLD J. ISBELL	GLENNON	MEREDITH	SARSFIELD
BAUSSELL	GURKE	NOA	SHELTON
BRINKLEY BASS	GYATT	ORLECK	STRIBLING
BROWNSON	HAMNER	OZBOURN	THEODORE E.
CHARLES H. ROAN	HAROLD J. ELLISON	PERRY	CHANDLER
CHARLES R. WARE	HENDERSON	POWER	VOGELGESANG
CONE	HOLLISTER	RICHARD B. ANDERSON	WARRINGTON
EVERSOLE	JAMES E. KYES	RICHARD E. KRAUS	WILLIAM C. LAWE
FLOYD B. PARKS	JOHN R. CRAIG	ROBERT H. McCARD	WILTSIE
FORREST ROYAL	JOHNSTON	ROWAN	WITEK
GEARING	JOSEPH P. KENNEDY, Jr.	RUPERTUS	

Representing the ultimate Second World War development of the American destroyer, these "Gearing" class ships incorporated lessons learnt in four years of Pacific warfare. The former pole mast was replaced by a tripod to carry the radar assembly, and the 40-mm. guns were replaced by six 3-inch guns. *Witek* became experimental with "pumpjet" propulsion in 1959. *Gyatt* was converted into a guided-missile destroyer in 1956, but the "Terrier" installation was removed in 1962. The others were converted for anti-submarine warfare under the FRAM (Fleet Rehabilitation and Modernisation) Programme with DASH (Drone Anti-Submarine Helicopter) platform.

Standard displacement	Full load displacement	Length	Beam	Draught
2,425 tons	3,479 tons	390½ feet	41 feet	19 feet

Main guns	Anti-aircraft guns	Anti-submarine weapons		
4–5 inch	Removed	1 ASROC 8-tube launcher, 2 triple torpedo launchers, 2 DASH		
	Gyatt and *Witek*: 4–3 inch	*Gyatt* and *Witek*: 2 triple torpedo launchers only		

Propelling machinery	Shaft horse power	Boilers	Speed	Complement
Geared steam turbines	60,000	4	34 knots	257 to 274

AGERHOLM

BENNER	EUGENE A. GREENE	HENRY W. TUCKER	PERKINS
BORDELON	EVERRET F. LARSEN	HERBERT J. THOMAS	ROGERS
CHARLES P. CECIL	FECHTELER	HIGBEE	SOUTHERLAND
CHEVALIER	FISKE	KENNETH D. BAILEY*	STEINAKER
CORRY	FRANK KNOX*	LEARY	STICKELL
DENNIS J. BUCKLEY	FURSE	McKEAN	TURNER*
DUNCAN*	GOODRICH*	MYLES C. FOX	VESOLE
DYESS	HANSON	NEWMAN K. PERRY	WILLIAM M. WOOD
ERNEST G. SMALL*	HAWKINS	O'HARE	WILLIAM R. RUSH

A development of the "Gearing" class, the necessity for radar picket destroyers arose in the later stages of war in the Pacific. Increasing aircraft speeds and suicide bombers demanded the greatest possible warning of approach, so these ships had their torpedo mountings removed and a tripod mainmast fitted to carry an imposing array of radar aerials. Ships were disposed in an extended screen many miles from the main fleet in order to give as early warning as possible of the approach of aircraft. In most ships the tripod mainmast was removed and the aerials mounted on the after superstructure. All the thirty-six ships listed above were completed in 1944–6. Six indicated (*) above remain radar pickets (DDR). The remainder underwent conversion to "straight" destroyers (26 FRAM I and 4 FRAM II) equipped with DASH (Drone Anti-submarine Helicopter) installation and variable depth sonar.

Standard displacement	Full load displacement	Length	Beam	Draught
2,425 tons	3,550 tons	390½ feet	41 feet	19 feet

Main guns	Anti-submarine weapons
4–5 inch (DDR: 6–5 inch)	1 ASROC 8-tube launcher, 2 triple torpedo launchers, 2 drone anti-submarine helicopters (2 fixed torpedo tubes in 4 ships instead of ASROC; 2 triple launchers only in DDR)

Propelling machinery	Shaft horse powe	Boilers	Speed	Complement
Geared steam turbines	60,000	4	34 knots	275

GOODRICH

ALFRED A. CUNNINGHAM	DE HAVEN	JAMES C. OWEN	PURDY
ALLEN M. SUMNER	DOUGLAS H. FOX	JOHN A. BOYLE	PUTNAM
AULT	ENGLISH	JOHN R. PIERCE	ROBERT K.
BARTON	FRANK E. EVANS	JOHN W. THOMASON	HUNTINGTON
BEATTY	GAINARD	JOHN W. WEEKS	SOLEY
BLUE	HANK	LAFFEY	STORMES
BORIE	HARLAN R. DICKSON	LOFBERG	STRONG
BRISTOL	HARRY E. HUBBARD	LOWRY	SAMUEL L. MOORE
BRUSH	HAYNSWORTH	LYMAN K. SWENSON	TAUSSIG
BUCK	HENLEY	MADDOX	WALDRON
CHARLES H. SPERRY	HUGH PURVIS	MANSFIELD	WALKE
COLLETT	HYMAN	MASSEY	WALLACE L. LIND
COMPTON	INGRAHAM	MOALE	WILLARD KEITH
		O'BRIEN	ZELLARS

Known as the "Allen M. Sumner" class, and constituting a shorter, earlier version of the "Gearing" type, these ships were the first twin turret destroyers in the American Navy. 33 of them underwent FRAM II conversion with DASH platform aft, and from these the quintuple torpedo tubes and 3-inch guns were removed. *Adams, Gwin, Harry F. Bauer, Henry A. Wiley, Lindsey, Robert H. Smith, Shannon, Shea, Thomas E. Fraser* and *Tolman*, originally of this class, are rated as destroyer minelayers (MMD).

Standard displacement	*Full load displacement*	*Length*	*Beam*	*Draught*
2,200 tons	3,320 tons	376½ feet	40¾ feet	19 feet

Main guns	*Anti-aircraft guns*	*Torpedo tubes*	*Anti-submarine weapons*	
6–5 inch	6–3 inch	5–21 inch	2 hedgehogs, 2 side-launching torpedo racks	

Propelling machinery	*Shaft horse power*	*Boilers*	*Speed*	*Complement*
Geared steam turbines	60,000	4 Babcock & Wilcox	34 knots	274

JOHN W. THOMASON

ALBERT W. GRANT	COGSWELL	JOHN WOOD	PICKING
BEARSS	COTTEN	KIDD	PORTER
BENNION	DASHIELL	KNAPP	PORTERFIELD
BLACK	GATLING	McNAIR	PRESTON
BULLARD	HALSEY POWELL	MARSHALL	REMEY
BRYANT	HEALY	MELVIN	STOCKHAM
CAPERTON	HOPEWELL	MERTZ	UHLMAN
CASSIN YOUNG	HUNT	NORMAN SCOTT	WEDDERBURN
CHAUNCEY	INGERSOLL		

Known as the Later "Fletcher" class, these vessels were practically identical with the original "Fletcher" class, the first war-construction destroyers built for the United States Navy. Some units still retain two sets of tubes, ten in all; a number of units lost the midships 5-inch gun and mount six 3-inch guns and a director in lieu of the 5-inch and 40-mm. mounts. Only reserve units retained 20 mm. A tripod foremast was fitted to take the weight of radar arrays. Of this class *Heywood L. Edwards* and *Richard P. Leary* were transferred to Japan in 1959; *Benham* to Peru in 1960; *Jarvis* and *McGowan* to Spain in 1960; *Cushing* to Brazil in 1961; *Dortch* to Argentina in 1961; *Rooks* and *Wadleigh* to Chile in 1962; *Clarence K. Bronson* and *Van Valkenburgh* to Turkey in 1967; *Lewis Hancock* and *Irwin* to Brazil in 1966 and 1968; *Charles J. Badger* and *Hickox* scheduled to Argentina. *Gregory* became port training ship in 1966 and renamed *Indoctrinator*. *Monssen* stricken 1963, *McDermut* broken up 1966, *Callahan* expended as target 1966.

Standard displacement	Full load displacement	Length	Beam	Draught
2,050 tons	3,050 tons	376¼ feet	39⅝ feet	18 feet

Main guns	Anti-aircraft guns	Torpedo tubes	Anti-submarine weapons
5–5 inch or 4–5 inch	10–40 mm. or 6–3 inch	5–21 inch (reserve ships)	2 Hedgehogs, 2 triple torpedoes

Propelling machinery	Shaft horse power	Boilers	Speed	Complement
Geared steam turbines	60,000	4 Babcock & Wilcox	35 knots	250

COTTEN

ABBOTT	HARADEN	METCALF	ROWE	TERRY
BELL	HARRISON	MILLER	SCHROEDER	THE SULLIVANS
BOYD	HART	MULLANY	SHIELDS	TRATHEN
BRAINE	HAZELWOOD	McCORD	SIGOURNEY	TWINING
BURNS	HUDSON	McKEE	SIGSBEE	WATTS
COWELL	IZARD	OWEN	STANLEY	WICKES
DALY	JOHN D. HENLEY	PAUL HAMILTON	STEPHEN POTTER	WILEY
FOOTE	JOHN RODGERS	PRICHETT	STEVENS	WREN
FRANKS	LA VALETTE	ROBINSON	STODDARD	YOUNG
HALFORD	LAWS	ROSS		

Original "Fletcher" class. Several were rearmed with 3-inch guns in lieu of smaller A.A. mounts. During the Second World War six were equipped with catapult and seaplane, some of the very few destroyers ever to be so equipped. Pole mast was replaced with tripod. In 1957–62 *Anthony, Charles Ausburn, Claxton, Dyson, Ringgold* and *Wadsworth* were transferred to the German Federal Republic, *Capps, Converse* and *David W. Taylor* to Spain, *Aulick, Bradford, Brown, Charrette, Conner* and *Hall* to Greece, and *Bennett, Guest* and *Hailey* to Brazil, *Hale* to Colombia, *Heerman* and *Stembel* to Argentina, *Isherwood* to Peru, and *Ammen, Fullam* and *Howorth* were disposed of. *Erben* was transferred to Korea in 1963, *Yarnall* to Brazil in 1966, *Kimberley* to Taiwan China in 1967. *Killen* was stricken in 1963, *Smalley* in 1965, *Tingey* in 1966.

Standard displacement	Full load displacement	Length	Beam	Draught
2,1 00 tons	3,050 tons	376¼ feet	39⅔ feet	18 feet

Main guns	Anti-aircraft guns	Torpedo tubes	Anti-submarine weapons	
5 or 4–5 inch	6–40 mm. or 6–3 inch	5–21 inch (reserve ships)	2 fixed Hedgehogs, 2 triple torpedoes	

Propelling machinery	Shaft horse power	Boilers	Speed	Complement
Geared steam turbines	60,000	4 Babcock & Wilcox	35 knots	249

HAZLEWOOD

BEALE	EATON	NICHOLAS	RADFORD	TAYLOR
CONWAY	FLETCHER	O'BANNON	RENSHAW	WALKER
CONY	JENKINS	PHILIP	SPROSTON	WALLER

Former standard destroyers of the "Fletcher" class, 18 ships were converted to provide close support units for convoy escorts, with some slight differences between ships: one vessel no tubes, various others not fitted with later pattern tripod foremast. This class had a comprehensive anti-submarine armament including an ahead-throwing rocket launcher in place of the former "B" turret, or a trainable hedgehog, a depth charge rack, two side-launching torpedo racks, and two fixed Hedgehogs installed on the port and starboard sides of the forward shelter deck below the bridge wings. *Sauffley* was equipped as an experimental escort destroyer (EDDE) with one 5-inch gun, two 3-inch anti-aircraft guns and no torpedo tubes. All the ships listed above were completed in 1942–3. *Jenkins*, *Nicholas* and *Radford* underwent FRAM II conversion (Fleet Rehabilitation and Modernisation) in 1960, with DASH, helodeck and hangar for two drones, and ASW torpedo launchers, a nest of three on each side; and the 3-inch guns were removed. *Jenkins* is fitted with VDS (variable depth sonar) on the stern. The whole class were again redesignated as DD in 1962. *Murray* was stricken from the Navy List in 1965, *Sauffley* was expended as a target in 1968, and *Bache* was wrecked after running aground off Rhodes, Greece in 1968 and stricken from the Navy List.

Standard displacement	Full load displacement	Length	Beam	Draught
2,080 tons	2,940 tons	376¼ feet	39⅔ feet	18 feet

Main guns	Anti-aircraft guns	Anti-submarine weapons		
2–5 inch dual purpose	4–3 inch (except FRAM)	1 rocket launcher, 2 triple side torpedo racks, 2 fixed Hedgehogs		

Propelling machinery	Shaft horse power	Boilers	Speed	Complement
Geared steam turbines	60,000	4 Babcock & Wilcox	35 knots	249

RADFORD

CARMICK	EDWARDS	GHERARDI	JEFFERS	QUICK	THOMPSON
COWIE	ENDICOTT	GLEAVES	KEARNEY	SATTERLEE	THORN
DAVISON	ERICSSON	GRAYSON	McCOOK	STEVENSON	TILLMAN
DORAN	FITCH	HAMBLETON	MERVINE	STOCKTON	WILKES
DOYLE	FRANKFORD	HERNDON	NIBLACK	SWANSON	WOOLSEY
EARLE					

BAILEY	CHARLES F. HUGHES	GANSEVOORT	LAUB	MAYO	NIELDS
BANCROFT	COGHLAN	GILLESPIE	McLANAHAN	MEADE	ORDRONAUX
BOYLE	FARENHOLT	HOBBY	MACKENZIE	MURPHY	PARKER
CHAMPLIN	FRAZIER	KALK	MADISON		

Eleven former units of the "Gleaves" class were transferred to the Turkish, Italian, Greek, Taiwan and Japanese navies. *Baldwin* was stricken in 1961, *Edison* in 1966, *Knight* in 1967, *Nelson* and *Welles* in 1968. The ships of this type converted to High-Speed Minesweepers (DMS), with the removal of one after 5-inch gun and the torpedo tubes, reverted to destroyer status and designation in 1955. A similar type of ships are the "Mayo" class. One vessel of this earlier type transferred to Italy, and two to Taiwan China, *Caldwell* was stricken in 1965 and *Kendrick* in 1966.

Standard displacement ("31 Gleaves" class) 1,700 tons ("22 Mayo" class) 1,620 tons	*Full load displacement* 2,580 tons 2,575 tons	*Length* 348¼ feet	*Beam* 36 feet 35⅓ feet	*Draught* 18 feet
Main guns 4–5 inch 3–5 inch (ex-DMS)	*Anti-aircraft guns* 4–40 mm., 7–20 mm.	*Torpedo tubes* 5 or 10–21 inch	*Complement* 230 to 240	
Propelling machinery Geared steam turbines	*Shaft horse power* 50,000	*Boilers* 4 Babcock & Wilcox	*Speed* 34 knots	

THOMPSON

10 "KASHIN" CLASS

Unlike the destroyer-cruisers of the "Kresta" and "Kynda" classes (see earlier pages), which have a break in the forecastle deck at the quarter deck, the "Kashin" class are flush decked vessels, and they have a pronounced lift forward combined with an acute cut-water bow. They are an entirely new class of guided missile armed super-destroyers of quite unusual and futuristic looking design with special anti-aircraft and anti-submarine propensities. Their appearance is most striking with very fine lines giving an impression of litheness and high speed. They have four separate towers carrying radars for missile guidance, anti-aircraft direction, search, and gunnery direction. There are believed to be a total of at least six completed ships of this class, including two units built in the Baltic and two vessels in the Black Sea, but others are understood to be on the stocks, and the class seems likely to run into series production. "Kashin" class destroyers bearing the numbers 11, 078, 296, 363 and 381 have been observed, and the following names have been published: *Boikii, Obraztsovy, Provorny, Provedyonny, Slavny, Soobrazityelny* and *Steregushchy*.

Standard displacement	Full load displacement	Length	Beam	Draught
4,300 tons	5,200 tons	475 feet	53 feet	19 feet

Guided weapons	Guns	Anti-submarine armament	Torpedo tubes	Aircraft
2 twin launchers for s-to-a	4–3.3 inch (2 twin)	4 12-barrel launchers	5–21 inch	Helicopter

Propelling machinery	Shaft horse power	Speed	Mines	Complement
4 gas turbines	100,000	35 knots	Fitted for	390

"KASHIN" class

10 "KRUPNY" CLASS

Known as the "Plamyonny" class in the Soviet Navy and as the "Krupny" class by NATO code designation, these are a novel type of flush-decked destroyers designed to carry large guided missile launchers forward and aft. They are long, slim and low-lying, and they have an attenuated, lithe and rakish appearance without a preponderance of heavy or block superstructure, but their sea-to-air/sea launchers for short range guided missiles, mounted on the forecastle and on the quarter deck are most conspicuous. They have a helicopter spot landing platform built as an open pier on the stern. Initial construction of the class is said to have commenced in 1958 at Leningrad. It was understood that there were originally to have been twelve vessels of the class, but it is believed that construction was discontinued in favour of successive improved types. Later units were also reported to be fitted with surface-to-surface guided missile launchers. Two were converted to carry surface-to-air missiles in 1967. Ships of this class numbered 185, 229, 372, 526, 700 and 703 have been observed, but the names recorded are *Gordy*, *Gremyashchy* and *Plamyonny*.

Standard displacement	Full load displacement	Length	Beam	Draught
3,650 tons	4,650 tons	453 feet	44 feet	16½ feet

Guided weapons	Guns	Anti-submarine armament	Torpedo tubes	Aircraft
2 launchers for s-to-s	16–57 mm. (4 quadruple)	2 16-barrel launchers	6–21 inch (2 triple)	Helicopter

Propelling machinery	Boilers	Shaft horse power	Speed	Complement
Geared steam turbines	4	80,000	34 knots	360

"KRUPNY' class

6 "KILDIN" CLASS   2 "KOTLIN" SAM CLASS

The "Kildin" class are large destroyers with the "Kotlin" type hull redesigned at a very early stage as guided missile armed destroyers, with a launcher installed in place of the after gun mountings. Their identification as the "Kildin" class is by NATO designation. The first of the class, squat and racy in appearance, but withal much heavier looking and more built up aft, is reported to have commissioned in 1958. At least one of the completed units are reported to be in the Baltic Fleet. Nos. 165 and others have been observed.

The "Kotlin" SAM class are basically standard destroyers of the "Kotlin" class modified with a twin "Goa" launcher for surface-to-air guided missiles installed aft on the shelter deck, taking the place of the main twin gun turret, and the anti-aircraft guns reduced to one quadruple mounting. The two units of the "Kotlin" class recast to the new design are reported to have completed conversion to launch surface-to-air missiles the first in 1960 and second in 1966.

	Standard displacement	Full load displacement	Length	Beam	Draught
"Kotlin" SAM Class:	2,850 tons	3,885 tons	425 feet	41½ feet	16½ feet
"Kildin" Class:	3,000 tons	4,000 tons	426½ feet	42⅔ feet	15½ feet

	Guided weapons	Guns	Torpedo tubes	Anti-submarine weapons
"Kotlin" SAM Class:	s-to-a launcher aft	2–5.1 inch, 4–57 mm. A.A.	3–21 inch	6 side-thrown D.C. projectors
"Kildin" Class:	s-to-a launcher aft	16–57 mm. A.A.	6–21 inch	2 16-barrel rocket launchers

	Propelling machinery	Shaft horse power	Boilers	Speed	Complement
"Kotlin" SAM Class:	Geared steam turbines	80,000	4 high pressure	36 knots	285
"Kildin" Class:	Geared steam turbines	80,000	4 high pressure	35 knots	300

"KILDIN" class

KOTLIN SAM class

"TALLINN" class

25 "KOTLIN" CLASS   1 "TALLINN" CLASS

The prototope of this new flush-decked semi-leader or fleet type of large destroyers was first observed about 1955. Known as the "Tallinn" class, the first unit carried several pennant numbers including 76 and 778. The displacement of 3,200 tons standard and 4,300 tons full load was more than that of the evolved "Kotlin" class. The 5.1-inch guns in two turrets, including firing directors, are fully stabilised. This was the first time that such an armament had been contrived in a ship of destroyer size, an experiment in top weight.

The "Kotlin" class, reported to number twenty-five units, are improved versions of the "Tallinn" type with similar hulls but differing features. This new class of fast anti-aircraft and anti-submarine destroyers was apparently designed for mass production, numbers observed including 32, 75, 77, 78, 79, 82, 86, 95, 502 and 774. In some ships the six depth charge throwers are mounted on rotating platforms on the stern. Particulars of the "Kotlin" class are given below.

Many units of the "Kotlin" class have been modernised under a programme similar to the U.S. Navy's FRAM programme, with extensive modifications in anti-submarine warfare, electronics and anti-aircraft armament. Several of the class are fitted with a helicopter platform abaft the after mounting, and two ships are fitted with a surface-to-air twin missile launcher aft.

Standard displacement	Full load displacement	Length	Beam	Draught
2,850 tons	3,885 tons	425 feet	41½ feet	16 feet

Main guns	Anti-aircraft guns	Torpedo tubes	Anti-submarine armament	
4–5.1 inch	16–45 mm.	10–21 inch	6 side-thrown depth charge projectors	

Propelling machinery	Shaft horse power	Boilers	Speed	Complement
Geared steam turbines	80,000	4	36 knots	285

"KOTLIN" class

BEZSMENNI	OZHIVLYONNY	SMYSHLYONI	SPOSOBNI	SUROVI
BEZUKORIZNYONNI	SERDITI	SOKRUSHYTELNI	STATNI	SVOBODNI
OCHAYANNI	SERYOZNI	SOLIDNI	STEPYONNI	VDUMCHYVI
OTVETSVENNI	SMELI	SOOBRAZITYELNI	STOYKI	VRAZUMITYELNI
OZHESTOCHONNI	SMOTRYASHCHI	SOVERSHENNI	STREMITYELNI	

The "Skory" class destroyers are, like all major Soviet warships, equipped for minelaying. Handsome-looking vessels with a low raking silhouette, the first units were observed during 1953. Up to thirty names formerly reported are uncertain but the above are believed to be reliable: some ships may be numbered only. There were to have been 85 destroyers of this class, but their construction beyond 75 units is reported to have been discontinued in favour of later types of destroyers and after various transfers to other navies it is understood that not more than 55 vessels of this class remain. Many units of the "Skory" class have been identified under a fleet rehabilitation and modernisation programme with extensive alterations to anti-aircraft armament, electronics and anti-submarine weapons. The names of "Skory" class destroyers are apparently based on their fleet assignment. Those in the Black Sea have names beginning with B, those in the northern Fleet with O, in the Baltic with S, and Pacific V.

Standard displacement	Full load displacement	Length	Beam	Draught
2,600 tons	3,500 tons	420 feet	41 feet	15 feet

Main guns	Anti-aircraft guns	Torpedo tubes	Mines	Anti-submarine weapons
4–5.1 inch	2–3 inch, 7 or 8–37 mm.	10–21 inch	80	4 Depth charge throwers

Propelling machinery	Shaft horse power	Boilers	Speed	Complement
Geared turbines	70,000	4	36 knots	260

SVOBODNI

DESTROYERS

France

BOUVET   **DU CHAYLA**   **JAUREGUIBERRY**   **MAILLE BREZE**
CASABIANCA   **DUPETIT THOUARS**   **KERSAINT**   **SURCOUF**
CASSARD   **DUPERRE**   **LA BOURDONNAIS**   **TARTU**
CHEVALIER PAUL   **FORBIN**   **LA GALISSONIERE**   **VAUQUELIN**
D'ESTREES   **GUEPRATTE**

The first post-war French destroyers, these mounted the 57-mm. gun, a new French calibre, somewhat similar to the U.S. 3-inch gun. The 5-inch gun was adopted for the first time in the French Navy to facilitate ammunition supply, as it takes standard U.S. Navy ammunition. Formerly carried twelve torpedo tubes, six to fire the special anti-submarine homing torpedoes (retained) that home on any submarine in the vicinity, and six tubes to handle either anti-submarine or conventional torpedoes. The 5-inch armament is disposed with one turret forward on forecastle deck level and two aft. The last ship of this group of 18 units, *La Galissoniere*, of the anti-submarine type, was designed as a command ship and squadron leader, and has a reduced main armament of two 3.9-inch automatic anti-aircraft guns, but carries a helicopter and "Malafon" guided weapons. *Forbin*, *Jaureguiberry*, *La Bourdonnais* and *Tartu* are of the aircraft direction type for use as radar picket destroyers (*Duperré* of this type is now experimental). Of the twelve of the anti-aircraft type, four were re-armed with "Tartar" guided weapons, five with "Malafon" and three converted to command ships. All except *La Galissoniere* (in 1962) were completed in 1955–58.

Standard displacement	Full load displacement	Length	Beam	Draught
2,750 tons	3,750 to 3,910 tons	422 to 435⅔ feet	41⅓ to 42⅓ feet	17¾ to 18¼ feet

Main guns	Anti-aircraft guns	Guided weapons	Torpedo tubes	Anti-submarine weapons
6–5 inch exc. GM ships	4 to 6–57 mm., 2 to 6–20 mm.	1 launcher for "Malafon" (A/S)	6–21.7 inch	Depth charge mortars
2–3.9 inch in A/S ships	except A/S ships	or "Tartar" missiles (GM)		or rocket launchers

Propelling machinery	Shaft horse power	Boilers	Speed	Complement
Geared steam turbines	63,000	4	34 knots	281 to 336

KERSAINT

IMPAVIDO	IMPETUOSO	INDOMITO	INTREPIDO

Impetuoso and *Indomito*, first destroyers designed and built in Italy since the end of the Second World War, are large vessels with special anti-submarine and anti-aircraft armament, rated as *Caccio Torpediniere* and designated DD. On sea trials they attained a speed of 35 knots at full load. The armament of *Impavido* and *Intrepido* includes a "Tartar" surface-to-air guided missile launcher aft; provision was made for carrying a light anti-submarine helicopter and the machinery is of different type. They are designated DDG, and classed as *Caccia Lanciamissili*

	Standard displacement	Full load displacement	Length	Beam	Draught
Impetuoso, Indomito:	2,775 tons	3,811 tons	418¾ feet	43⅓ feet	17½ feet
Impavido, Intrepido:	3,201 tons	3,941 tons	429½ feet	44⅔ feet	14¾ feet

Main guns	Anti-aircraft guns	Torpedo tubes	Anti-submarine weapons	Guided weapons
4–5 inch	16–40 mm.	2 triple A/S	1 triple mortar	
2–5 inch	4–3 inch	2 triple A/S	4 single howitzers	Twin "Tartar" launcher

Propelling machinery	Shaft horse power	Boilers	Speed	Complement
Geared steam turbines	65,000	4 Foster-Wheeler	34 knots	393
Geared steam turbines	70,000	4	33.5 knots	344

Name	No.	Begun	Launched	Completed	Builders
IMPAVIDO	D 570	10 June 1957	25 May 1962	16 Nov. 1963	Cantieri del Tirreno, Riva Trigoso
INTREPIDO	D 571	16 May 1959	21 Oct. 1962	30 Oct. 1964	Ansaldo, Leghorn (formerly O.T.O. Yard)
IMPETUOSO	D 558	7 May 1952	16 Sept. 1956	25 Jan. 1958	Cantieri del Tirreno, Riva Trigoso
INDOMITO	D 559	24 Apr. 1952	7 Aug. 1955	23 Feb. 1958	Ansaldo, Leghorn (formerly O.T.O. Yard)

Note: Two other Italian destroyers are the *Artigliere* (ex-U.S.S. *Woodworth*) and *Aviere* (ex-U.S.S. *Nicholson*) of the "Gleaves" and "Mayo" classes, respectively, particulars of which are given in the U.S. pages.

Two more guided missile armed destroyers, *Ardito* and *Audace*, are under construction: 4,400 tons full load; 446½ × 46⅔ × 15 feet; 2 light A/S helicopters; 1 "Tartar" missile launcher; 2–5 inch and 4–3 inch guns; 6 A/S torpedo tubes; 4 boilers; 2 geared turbines, 73,000 s.h.p. = 33 knots.

IMPAVIDO

GELDERLAND NOORD BRABANT AMSTERDAM GRONINGEN FRIESLAND ROTTERDAM
HOLLAND ZEELAND DRENTHE LIMBURG OVERIJSSEL UTRECHT

The anti-submarine vessels of the "Holland" class, comprising *Gelderland, Holland, Noord Brabant* and *Zeeland*, were the first destroyers built for the Royal Netherlands Navy after the Second World War. They were begun in 1950–51, launched in 1953, and completed in 1954–55. The succeeding group of eight ships constitute the "Friesland" class. These larger fleet escorts have some side armour as well as deck protection, like light cruisers. Named after the provinces of Northern and Southern Holland and the two principal cities, they were begun in 1951–55, launched in 1953–56 and completed in 1956–58. Unlike most standard destroyers these two classes have no torpedo tubes, but they have "Limbo" type four-barrelled anti-submarine rocket throwers or depth charge mortars. Their 4.7-inch guns are fully automatic and radar controlled, and have a rate of fire of 50 rounds per minute. The special features of these ships are the large radar aerials surmounting the squat lattice masts, and the cowled fore funnel curving back from inside the foremast.

Standard displacement	Full load displacement	Length	Beam	Draught
"Holland" class 2,215 tons	2,765 tons	371 feet	$37\frac{1}{2}$ feet	$16\frac{3}{4}$ feet
"Friesland" class 2,497 tons	3,070 tons	$380\frac{1}{2}$ feet	$38\frac{1}{2}$ feet	17 feet

Main guns	Anti-aircraft guns	Anti-submarine weapons	Complement
4–4.7 inch	1–40 mm.	2–4 barrelled depth charge mortars	247
4–4.7 inch	6–40 mm.	2–4 barrelled depth charge mortars	284

Propelling machinery	Shaft horse power	Boilers	Speed
Geared steam turbines	45,000	4 Yarrow	32 knots
Geared steam turbines	60,000	4 controlled superheat	36 knots

Builders:—Dok-en-Werfmaatschappij Wilton-Fijenoord, Schiedam: *Gelderland* and *Overijssel*; Koninklijke Maatschappij De Schelde, Flushing: *Limburg, Noord Brabant, Utrecht* and *Zeeland*; Nederlandse Dok en Scheepsbouw Mij., Amsterdam: *Amsterdam, Drenthe, Friesland* and *Groningen*; Rotterdamse Droogdok Mij., Rotterdam: *Holland* and *Rotterdam*.

FRIESLAND

HALLAND	GASTRIKLAND	ÖSTERGÖTLAND
SMALAND	HALSINGLAND	SODERMANLAND

Halland and *Smaland* were the first Swedish destroyers of post-Second World War design. They have fully automatic gun turrets, ahead throwing anti-submarine weapons on the forecastle, low silhouette, massive block bridge tower, and truncated conical funnels. The remaining four ships have basically the same characteristics but with somewhat thinner funnels, flush-deck, and the mainmast stepped before the after funnel, whereas the "Halland" class have a forecastle and a diminutive mainmast well abaft the after funnel.

Standard displacement	Full load displacement	Length	Beam	Draught
Halland, Smaland, 2,650 tons	3,200 tons	397¼ feet	41½ feet	14¾ feet
Other four 2,150 tons	2,600 tons	380 feet	36¾ feet	12 feet

Main guns	Anti-aircraft guns	Guided weapons	Torpedo tubes	Anti-submarine weapons
4–4.7 inch	2–57 mm., 6–40 mm.	1 "Robot"	8–21 inch	2–4 barrelled depth charge mortars
4–4.7 inch	4 to 7–40 mm.	4 "Seacat"	6–21 inch	1–3 barrelled depth charge mortar

Propelling machinery	Shaft horse power	Boilers	Speed	Complement
Geared steam turbines	58,000	2	35 knots	290
Geared steam turbines	40,000	2	35 knots	244

Name	No.	Begun	Launched	Completed	Builders
HALLAND	J 18	1 Jan. 1951	16 July 1952	8 June 1955	Gotaverken, Goteborg
SMALAND	J 19	1 Jan. 1951	23 Oct. 1952	12 Jan. 1956	Eriksberg Mekaniska Verkstad
GASTRIKLAND	J 22	1 Oct. 1955	6 June 1956	14 Jan. 1959	Gotaverken, Goteborg
HALSINGLAND	J 23	1 Oct. 1955	14 Jan. 1957	17 June 1959	Kockums Mekaniska Verkstads
OSTERGOTLAND	J 20	1 Sept. 1955	8 May 1956	3 Mar. 1958	Gotaverken, Goteborg
SODERMANLAND	J 21	1 June 1955	28 May 1956	27 June 1959	Eriksberg Mekaniska Verkstad

Note: There are also the destroyers *Oland* and *Uppland*, 2,000 tons completed in 1947–48; *Halsingborg, Kalmar, Sundsvall* and *Visby*, 1,150 tons, completed in 1943–44 (see full particulars and photographs on pages 174 to 177 of the 1960 Edition), re-rated as frigates in 1965; and *Gavle* and *Karlskrona* 1,250 tons, completed in 1940–41, re-rated as frigates in 1961.

ÖSTERGÖTLAND

| **BAYERN** | **HAMBURG** | **HESSEN** | **SCHLESWIG-HOLSTEIN** |

These are the first destroyers built for the *Bundesmarine* or Federal German Navy and, apart from the training ship *Deutschiand*, are the biggest warships built in West Germany since the Second World War. Named after the countries of the Federal German Republic, they have a powerful yet handsome appearance, and are very comprehensively armed and equipped, with a good turn of speed. Three guided missile armed destroyers of the "Charles" F. Adams" class are being built in U.S.A. for West Germany.

Standard displacement	Full load displacement	Length	Beam	Draught
3,400 tons	4,400 tons	439¾ feet	44 feet	17¼ feet

Main guns	Anti-aircraft guns	Anti-submarine weapons	Torpedo tubes
4–3.9 inch (100 mm.) dual purpose (single)	8–40 mm. (4 twin)	2 four-barrelled depth charge mortars (Bofors rocket launchers)	5–21 inch and 2 for ASW

Propelling machinery	Shaft horse power	Boilers	Speed	Complement
Geared steam turbines	68,000	4 Wahodag	35 knots	282

Name	No.	Begun	Launched	Completed	Builders
BAYERN	D 183	1961	14 Aug. 1962	6 July 1965	H. C. Stülcken Sohn, Hamburg
HAMBURG	D 181	1959	26 Mar. 1960	23 Mar. 1964	H. C. Stülcken Sohn, Hamburg
HESSEN	D 184	1962	4 May 1963	31 Oct. 1968	H. C. Stülcken Sohn, Hamburg
SCHLESWIG-HOLSTEIN	D 182	1959	20 Aug. 1960	12 Oct. 1964	H. C. Stülcken Sohn, Hamburg

(The Federal German Navy also had six former United States destroyers, namely Z 1 (ex-U.S.S. *Anthony*), Z 2 (ex-U.S.S. *Ringgold*), Z 3 (ex-U.S.S. *Wadsworth*), Z 4 (ex-U.S.S. *Claxton*), Z 5 (ex-U.S.S. *Dyson*), and Z 6 (ex-U.S.S. *Charles Ausburn*), all of the "Fletcher" class and lent in 1958-60, but Z 6 was discarded in 1968).

Note: The training ship *Deutschland* was the first West German naval ship to exceed the post-war limit of 3,000 tons displacement. Of the large destroyer/small cruiser type, she has a displacement of 4,880 tons standard and 5,500 tons full load with a length of 475¾ feet, beam of 59 feet and draught of 16 feet. Guns: 4–3.9 inch, 6–40 mm. A/S weapons: 2 4-barrelled depth charge mortars. Aircraft: 1 helicopter. Machinery: 2 Mercedes-Benz and 2 Maybach diesels, B.H.P. 6,680 and geared steam turbines, S.H.P. 8,000. 3 shafts. Speed: 21.9 kts. Complement 565. Begun 1959. Launched 5 Nov. 1960. Completed 1963.

BAYERN

KIKUZUKI	**ASAGUMO**	**AMATSUKAZE**
MOCHIZUKI	**MAKIGUMO**	
TAKATSUKI	**MINEGUMO**	
	YAMAGUMO	

The three vessels of the Improved "Zuki" or "Moon" class are fleet destroyers of striking appearance evidently inspired by the design of contemporary American destroyer leaders and escort ships. They are each equipped with a drone anti-submarine helicopter and hangar. *Kikuzuki, Mochizuki* and *Takatsuki* were completed in 1968, 1969 and 1967, respectively. A fourth ship of this class was ordered under the 1966 construction programme.

The four units of the "Gumo" or "Cloud" class are smaller and more lightly armed diesel powered vessels of the anti-submarine escort type. They were completed in 1966 and 1968.

The larger ship *Amatsukaze* was the largest naval vessel completed in Japan after the Second World War and the first to be armed with guided missiles. Distinguished by clean lines, flush deck and minimum of superstructure, she is equipped with surface to air guided missiles supplied from the U.S.A. and designed to carry and operate a helicopter.

Two helicopter destroyers of 4,700 tons, a guided missile destroyer of 3,900 tons and three destroyers of 2,000 tons are being built or projected under the third five-year construction programme, 1968 to 1972.

	Standard displacement	*Full load displacement*	*Length*	*Beam*	*Draught*
Improved "Zuki" class:	3,000 tons	3,900 tons	446¼ feet	44 feet	14½ feet
"Gumo" class:	2,000 tons	2,650 tons	374 feet	38¾ feet	12¾ feet
Amatsukaze:	3,050 tons	4,000 tons	429¾ feet	44 feet	13⅓ feet

	Guns	*Guided weapons*	*Torpedo launchers*	*Anti-submarine weapons*
Improved "Zuki" class:	2–5 inch (single)		6–12 inch (2 triple) homing	ASROC, DASH, 1-4 barrel mortar
"Gumo" class:	4–3 inch (2 twin)		6–12 inch (2 triple) homing	ASROC, 1–4 barrel mortar
Amatsukaze:	4–3 inch (2 twin)	"Tartar" launcher (single)	6–12 inch (2 triple) homing	Helicopter, 2 Hedgehogs

	Propelling machinery	*Boilers*	*Shaft horse power*	*Speed*	*Complement*
Improved "Zuki" class:	Geared steam turbines	2 high pressure	60,000	32 knots	270
"Gumo" class:	Diesels		26,500	27 knots	210
Amatsukaze:	Geared steam turbines	2 high pressure	60,000	33 knots	290

TAKATSUKI

YAMAGUMO

AMATSUKAZE

SHIKINAMI

MURASAME

AKIZUKI	HARUSAME	AYANAMI	SHIKINAMI	HARUKAZE
TERUZUKI	MURASAME	ISONAMI	TAKANAMI	YUKIKAZE
	YUDACHI	MAKINAMI	URANAMI	
		ONAMI		

The two ships of the "Zuki" or "Moon" class were destroyers of a new design with a long forecastle hull. Received from U.S.A. as part of the Military Aid Programme, but built in Japanese shipyards under an "off-shore" procurement agreement. They were designed as flotilla leaders to serve as senior officers' ships, and *Akizuki* became the flagship of the "Maritime Self-Defence Force", as Japan's post-war navy is still known.

The two vessels of the "Same" or "Rain" class were designed as anti-aircraft destroyers. Although of typically Japanese appearance there is a suggestion of American influence in their layout.

The seven destroyers of the "Nami" or "Wave" class were designed as anti-submarine escorts. The "Hedgehog" throwers are mounted on turntables before the bridge; four torpedo loading racks are mounted in pairs abreast the after funnel; and droppers for anti-submarine homing torpedoes are mounted on the quarter deck.

The two vessels of the "Kaze" or "Wind" class were the first destroyer-hulled ships built in Japan after the Second World War. In construction electric welding was used, with high tension steel in the hull and light alloy in the superstructure.

Japan also has four ex-U.S. destroyers, the *Ariake* and *Yugure* of the later "Fletcher" class, and the *Asakaze* and *Hatakaze* of the "Gleaves" class.

Standard displacement	Full load displacement	Length	Beam	Draught
"Zuki" class: 2,350 tons	2,890 tons	387¼ feet	39½ feet	13½ feet
"Same" class: 1,800 tons	2,500 tons	354½ feet	36 feet	12¼ feet
"Nami" class: 1,700 tons	2,500 tons	357¾ feet	35½ feet	11⅞ feet
"Kaze" class: 1,700 tons	2,340 tons	358½ feet	34½ feet	12 feet

Main and anti-aircraft guns	Torpedo tubes, launchers	Anti-submarine weapons
3–5 inch d.p.; 4–3 inch A.A.	4–21 inch (quad), 2 homing	2 Hedgehogs, 2 Y-guns, 1 rocket launcher
3–5 inch d.p.; 4–3 inch A.A.	8 short anti-submarine	1 Hedgehog, 2 Y-guns, 1 D.C. rack
6–3 inch A.A. (3 twin)	4–21 inch (quad), 2 homing	2 Hedgehogs, 2 Y-guns
3–5 inch d.p.; 8–40 mm. A.A.	Tubes for short homing	2 Hedgehogs, 4 K-guns, 1 D.C. rack

Propelling machinery	Shaft horse power	Boilers	Speed	Complement
Geared steam turbines	45,000	2 high pressure	32 knots	330
Geared steam turbines	30,000	2 high pressure	30 knots	250
Geared steam turbines	35,000	2 high pressure	32 knots	230
Geared steam turbines	30,000	2 high pressure	30 knots	240

AKIZUKI

ALP ARSLAN   KILIÇ ALI PASA   MARESAL FEVZI CAKMAK   PIYALE PAŞA

These four ships were formerly the British destroyers *Matchless*, *Milne*, *Marne* and *Meteor*, respectively, survivors of a class of eight, one of the most successful and handsome types which ever served in the Royal Navy. They were the first British destroyers to have three power-worked turrets. *Milne* was fitted as the flotilla leader. All four ships were transferred from Great Britain to Turkey under an agreement signed in Ankara on 16th August 1957 and were delivered to Turkey after refit in Great Britain in 1958–59, when the after bank of four 21-inch torpedo tubes and the secondary armament of one 4-inch gun and ten 20-mm. anti-aircraft guns were removed and replaced by a deckhouse, a triple-barrelled "Squid" depth charge mortar and six 40-mm. Bofors anti-aircraft guns; and they were renamed after famous generals and 16-18th century admirals.

Standard displacement	Full load displacement	Length	Beam	Draught
2,115 tons	2,840 tons	362½ feet	36¾ feet	16¼ feet

Main guns	Anti-aircraft guns	Torpedo tubes	Anti-submarine weapons
6–4.7 inch	6–40 mm.	4–21 inch	1 "Squid" triple-barrelled depth charge mortar

Propelling machinery	Shaft horse power	Boilers	Speed	Complement
Geared steam turbines	48,000	2 Admiralty 3-drum type	36 knots	240

Name	No.	Begun	Launched	Completed	Builders
ALP ARSLAN	D 348	24 Jan. 1940	30 Dec. 1941	6 Aug. 1942	Scotts' S.B. & Eng. Ltd., Greenock
KILIÇ ALI PASA	D 350	14 Sept. 1940	4 Sept. 1941	26 Feb. 1942	Alex. Stephen & Sons, Ltd., Govan
MARESAL FEVZI CAKMAK	D 349	23 Oct. 1939	30 Oct. 1940	2 Dec. 1941	Vickers-Armstrongs, Ltd., Tyne
PIYALE PAŞA	D 351	14 Sept. 1940	3 Nov. 1941	12 Aug. 1942	Alex. Stephen & Sons, Ltd., Govan

Note: Turkey also has six ex-U.S. destroyers, *Gaziantep*, *Gelibolu*, *Gemlik*, *Giresun*, *Istanbul* and *Izmir*. Of the four British-built destroyers, *Demirhisar*, *Muavenet* and *Sultanhisar* were discarded in 1960, and *Gayret* in 1965.

KILIC ALI PASA

RIVEROS   WILLIAMS

The layout and general arrangements in these two destroyers, named after Almirante Riveros and Almirante Williams, were strictly conventional with two funnels, but an unusual feature was the tapering tubular foremast. The main armament is disposed in four single gunhouses, two forward and two aft, "B" and "X" guns super-firing over "A" and "Y" positions; they are automatic with a range of 12,500 yards (or over seven miles) and an elevation of 75 degrees. Each ship also carries an anti-aircraft battery of six single 40-mm. guns, disposed three on each beam on an extension of the forecastle deck between the funnels. The torpedo tubes are in a quintuple bank abaft the after funnel; and the two "Squid" triple depth charge mortars are sited abreast the mainmast. The conventional power plant comprises Vickers-built Parsons turbines of "Pametrada' design turning two shafts. The operations room and similar spaces are air-conditioned. The radar was designed to work with new fire control systems developed by Vickers. There are twin rudders for manoeuvrability. Ventilation and heating systems were designed to suit the Chilean coastline, extending from the tropics to Cape Horn. Bunks are fitted for the entire crew. The electrical system is on alternating current; the galleys are all-electric; and there is fluorescent lighting. *Riveros* was completed within two years of her launch, but she was not handed over to Chile until 16 Feb. 1962.*   British "Seacat" radar controlled short range surface to air guided weapon systems were fitted at the Chilean Navy Yard at Talcahuano in 1964.

Standard displacement	Full load displacement	Length	Beam	Draught
2,730 tons	3,300 tons	402 feet	43 feet	13⅓ feet

Main guns	Anti-aircraft guns	Guided weapons	Anti-submarine weapons	Torpedo tubes
4–4 inch (single)	6–40 mm. (single)	1 quadruple launcher for "Seacat" missiles	2 "Squid" triple-barrelled depth charge mortars	5–21 inch (quintuple)

Propelling machinery	Shaft horse power	Boilers	Speed	Complement
Geared steam turbines	54,000	2 Babcock & Wilcox	34.5 knots	266

Name	No.	Begun	Launched	Completed	Builders
RIVEROS	DD 18	12 Apr. 1957	12 Dec. 1958	1 Dec. 1960*	Vickers-Armstrongs Ltd., Barrow
WILLIAMS	DD 19	20 June 1956	5 May 1958	26 Mar. 1960	Vickers-Armstrongs Ltd., Barrow

ALMIRANTE RIVEROS

ARAGUA   NUEVA ESPARTA   ZULIA

These three ships are among the most modern destroyers in the South American navies. They are recognitionally very similar to the British and Australian destroyers of the "Battle" type. In fact, the design would appear to be a combination of a "Daring" class armament and layout on a "Battle" class hull and appearance. Of considerable size, but they do not carry the complicated electronic equipment to be found in the ships of the larger navies and there is generous space below decks making provision for most comfortable and habitable quarters. *Aragua* was completed some time after the other two vessels had joined the Venezuelan Fleet. All three ships are air-conditioned throughout, with a comprehensive electrical system. *Nueva Esparta* and *Zulia* underwent a major refit at Vickers-Armstrongs (Shipbuilders) Limited, Palmers Hebburn Works for seven months in 1959, and British "Squid" anti-submarine depth charge mortars were mounted.

Standard displacement	*Full load displacement*	*Length*	*Beam*	*Draught*
2,600 tons	3,300 tons	402 feet	43 feet	12¾ feet

Main guns	*Anti-aircraft guns*	*Torpedo tubes*	*Anti-submarine weapons*	
6–4.5 inch	16–40 mm.	3–21 inch	"Squids", 2 depth charge throwers, 2 depth charge tracks	

Propelling machinery	*Shaft horse power*	*Boilers*	*Speed*	*Complement*
Geared steam turbines	50,000	2	34.5 knots	254

Name	*No.*	*Begun*	*Launched*	*Completed*	*Builders*
ARAGUA	D 31	29 June 1953	27 Jan. 1955	14 Feb. 1956	Vickers-Armstrongs, Barrow-in-Furness
NUEVA ESPARTA	D 11	24 July 1951	19 Nov. 1952	8 Dec. 1953	Vickers-Armstrongs, Barrow-in-Furness
ZULIA	D 21	24 July 1951	29 June 1953	15 Sept. 1954	Vickers-Armstrongs, Barrow-in-Furness

NUEVA ESPARTA

FRIGATES

THE appellation "frigate" was early adopted by the French for a particular type of fighting ship, and soon became the accepted term for the smaller, faster and more lightly armed vessel carrying her armament on one deck and intended to act as observer for the line-of-battle ship, but not to occupy a place in the line. In Britain, frigate was the name attached to light and speedy one-decked ships, a smaller type of vessel being known as a sloop which had its approximate equivalent in the French corvette. Frigates became a standard class of warship ranking next to ships of the line. They were used to obtain information as to the operations of enemy fleets, and to direct the movements of their own, but it was unusual for them to join in the line of battle, their clashes ordinarily occurring in actions with single ships of their own class. Nelson always complained bitterly of the lack of frigates (as did the admirals in both world wars). Frigate by his time were as useful and formidable scouts as were our fast reconnaissance warships of modern times. With the introduction of steam and the growth of the British Navy, frigates were developed more than any other class of warship, many of the largest vessels in the fleet belonging to this wide-embracing class. The famous *Warrior*, Britain's first iron-clad, displacing 9,000 tons, was originally rated as a frigate. "Frigate" continued to be used for this type of ship up to 1887 when the old *Raleigh* of 5,200 tons and other ships were still rated as frigates, but after that all the former frigates were rated as cruisers. Thereafter the term "frigate" lapsed for over 55 years. On 3 March 1943 it was officially announced that the name "frigate" was to be revived for a new class of warship. Of an enlarged corvette type and bearing a family likeness to the pre-war sloop, but built more on the lines of the escort destroyer, our first modern frigates, of the numerous "River" class, were described at the time by naval officers as the finest naval weapon yet invented against the U-boat. In essence they were still one-decked ships like the frigates of old. Numbering, with those built for the Royal Canadian Navy, some 120 units, they displaced 1,460 tons, heavier than our pre-war destroyers, and carried two 4-inch guns, ten 20-mm. A.A. guns and a Hedgehog at a speed of 20 knots. They were followed by a group of nearly 80 frigates of a new type known as the "Captains" class, built in American yards and in most respects similar to the United States destroyer escort types of 1,400 tons with three 3-inch guns and a speed of 24 knots (turbo-electric), or 1,150 tons with a speed of 20 knots (diesel-electric) and 21 American-built frigates of the "Colony" class similar to the original "River" class but of 1,318 tons with 3-inch guns and a speed of 18 knots (reciprocating). The British frigate category thenceforward was a very broad one embracing not only the frigates proper of the "Loch" and "Bay" classes but the former sloops of the "Black Swan" classes with six 4-inch guns, the former escort destroyers of the "Hunt" group with displacements up to 1,175 tons and speeds up to 30 knots, the former corvettes of the "Castle" class of 1,100 tons with a speed of $16\frac{1}{2}$ knots (term "corvette" had been revived on 4 July 1940 after a lapse of 53 years), and former destroyers of 1,730 tons with speeds of $36\frac{3}{4}$ knots. No fewer than 75 British frigates or vessels which would now be classified as frigates were lost during the 1939–45 war. Since 1955 Britain has built or is building 68 new frigates comprising 15 of highly specialised anti-submarine type ("Whitby" and "Rothesay" classes), twelve of utility anti-submarine type ("Blackwood" class), four of anti-aircraft type ("Leopard" class), four of aircraft direction type ("Salisbury" class), seven of general purpose type ("Ashanti" class) and 26 of general purpose and anti-submarine type ("Leander" class). As a type the modern frigate has come to stay. Evolved because the corvette could not do quite all that was required of it, the frigate has developed into a utility destroyer, in fact an ideal escort vessel, submarine killer, anti-aircraft ship, radar picket or aircraft direction ship and maid-of-all-work. In 1969 there are 70 frigates in the British Navy. Their counterparts in the U.S. Navy were formerly the destroyer escorts, but in 1955 the big U.S. destroyer leaders including *Norfolk* (former light cruiser) with speeds of 35 knots, were reclassified as frigates. The new nuclear powered guided missile "frigate" *Truxtun* displaces 8,200 tons. The wheel has thus turned full cycle with frigates as heavy as those of 82 years ago.

ACHILLES	ARGONAUT	CLEOPATRA	EURYALUS	JUPITER	PENELOPE
AJAX	AURORA	DANAE	GALATEA	LEANDER	PHOEBE
ANDROMEDA	BACCHANTE	DIDO	HERMIONE	MINERVA	SCYLLA
ARETHUSA	CHARYBDIS	DIOMEDE	JUNO	NAIAD	SIRIUS

H.M.S. *Leander*, completed in 1963, was the prototype of a more versatile class of frigates which differ from previous vessels of the type in that they are flush to the stern without the break to the quarter deck. The design of the "Leander" class was developed from that of the highly successful "Rothesay" and "Whitby" classes of frigates known as "Type 12", noted for manoeuvrability, performance at high speed, and seakeeping qualities. The same hull form was used in the "Leander" class. The main armament is directed by a fully automatic radar fire control and gun direction system. The secondary armament of 40 mm. guns in single mountings in the first seven ships built will be replaced by "Seacat" ship-to-air guided missile launchers and directors. All the ships are fitted with the latest equipment for detecting and attacking submarines. The dipping asdic, or variable depth sonar, as latterly known, greatly enhances their submarine hunting capabilities. The ships carry a helicopter for anti-submarine use (armed with homing torpedoes). Thus, although stemming from the preceding classes of anti-submarine frigates, the "Leander" class developed into all-round general purpose frigates. The improved bridge structure gives greater all-round visibility, especially astern, than in previous ships with enclosed bridges. In the operations room information is presented by semi-automatic techniques. A high standard of accommodation is provided for the ship's company, including bunk sleeping, separate dining halls and cafeteria messing. The ships have electric galleys, and are air conditioned in operational spaces and mess decks.

Standard displacement	Full load displacement	Length	Beam	Draught
2,450 tons	2,860 tons	372 feet	41 or 43 feet	18 feet

Main guns	Guided weapons	Anti-aircraft weapons	Anti-submarine weapons	Aircraft
2–4.5 inch (one twin)	1 quadruple launcher for "Seacat" missiles	2–40 mm. guns in early ships 2–20 mm. in missile ships	"Limbo" three-barrelled depth charge mortar	1 Wasp helicopter

Propelling machinery	Shaft horse power	Boilers	Speed	Complement	Completed
Geared steam turbines	30,000	2	30 knots	262	1963–71

LEANDER

PHOEBE

ROTHESAY

127

BERWICK	EASTBOURNE	LOWESTOFT	ROTHESAY	TORQUAY
BLACKPOOL	FALMOUTH	PLYMOUTH	SCARBOROUGH	WHITBY
BRIGHTON	LONDONDERRY	RHYL	TENBY	YARMOUTH

1st Rate frigates of anti-submarine "quality" type primarily designed for location and detection of submarines. Fitted with underwater hunting equipment and submarine-killing weapons of post-war development. Good sea-keeping qualities enable them to maintain high speed in rough seas. All named after seaside resorts, and officially listed as "Type 12". Officially considered the most useful class in the broad frigate and escort category ever put into service. With high forecastle and clean lines they ride well in a sea-way, and are exceptionally dry. The excellent enclosed bridge is spacious, with splendid vision and heated windows in the fore part an asset in Arctic waters. Internal communications within departments satisfied every demand, and siting of voice-pipes, call-ups and intercoms proved most convenient. The operations room was the finest ever put into comparatively small warships. Specially designed with the lightest possible structure. Planned for rapid construction in emergency. The earlier six units, *Blackpool* (lent to New Zealand in 1966), *Eastbourne*, *Scarborough*, *Tenby*, *Torquay* and *Whitby*, constitute the "Whitby" class and the other nine the "Rothesay" class, the design of which was modified. The twelve 21-inch torpedo tubes were suppressed. In 1966–68 *Rothesay* and *Yarmouth* were refitted on the lines of the "Leander" class, and the other seven ships will be similarly reconstructed as opportunity offers, involving the removal of the 40 mm. gun and one of the "Limbo" A/S mountings for the installation of the "Seacat" launcher and helicopter hangar and flight pad.

Standard displacement	Full load displacement	Length	Beam	Draught
2,150 to 2,200 tons	2,560 to 2,600 tons	370 feet	41 feet	17½ feet
Main guns	*Anti-aircraft armament*		*Anti-submarine weapons*	*Complement*
2–4.5 inch	2–40 mm. (1–40 mm. in "Rothesay" class, being replaced by "Seacat")		2 "Limbo" 3-barrelled depth charge mortars	221 or 235
Propelling machinery	*Shaft horse power*	*Boilers*	*Speed*	*Completed*
Geared steam turbines	30,000	2 Babcock & Wilcox	30 knots	May 1956 to Oct. 1961

LONDONDERRY

ASHANTI   ESKIMO   GURKHA   MOHAWK   NUBIAN   TARTAR   ZULU

General purpose frigates designed to fulfil economically all the various functions of frigates rather than to have an outstanding performance in any one specialised role, but capable of meeting the main escort requirements of anti-submarine protection, anti-aircraft defence, and aircraft direction. Known as the "Tribal" class, and officially listed as "Type 81". With their two funnels, general design and layout, and rakish appearance they are reminiscent of the destroyer type which they largely supersede as maids-of-all-work. Although conventional in armament they have a COSAG combined steam and gas turbine propulsion installation, comprising main boiler and single cylinder steam turbine of 12,500 s.h.p. combined with gas turbine of 7,500 h.p., both prime movers being located side by side in a machinery space forward of the gearing. Compartmental integrity enables each ship to be steamed through nuclear fall-out with the ship's company enclosed in an air-conditioned citadel and the power plant remotely controlled from a console in the centre of the ship.

Standard displacement	Full load displacement	Length	Beam	Draught
2,300 tons	2,700 tons	360 feet	42⅓ feet	17½ feet

Main guns	Guided weapons	Anti-aircraft guns	Anti-submarine weapons	Aircraft
2–4.5 inch dual purpose (single mountings)	2 quadruple launchers for "Seacat" missiles in *Zulu*	2–40 or 2–20 mm. (single mountings)	1 "Limbo" three-barrelled depth charge mortar	Wasp helicopter

Propelling machinery	Shaft horse power	Boilers	Speed	Complement
Combined steam and gas turbines	20,000	1 Babcock & Wilcox +1 auxiliary	28 knots	253

Name	No.	Begun	Launched	Completed	Builders
ASHANTI	F 117	15 Jan. 1958	9 Mar. 1959	23 Nov. 1961	Yarrow & Co. Ltd., Scotstoun
ESKIMO	F 119	22 Oct. 1958	20 Mar. 1960	21 Feb. 1963	J. Samuel White & Co. Ltd., Cowes
GURKHA	F 122	3 Nov. 1958	11 July 1960	13 Feb. 1963	John I. Thornycroft & Co. Ltd., Woolston
MOHAWK	F 125	23 Dec. 1960	5 Apr. 1962	29 Nov. 1963	Vickers-Armstrongs Ltd., Barrow
NUBIAN	F 131	7 Sept. 1959	6 Sept. 1960	9 Oct. 1962	H.M. Dockyard, Portsmouth
TARTAR	F 133	22 Oct. 1959	19 Sept. 1960	26 Feb. 1962	H.M. Dockyard, Devonport
ZULU	F 124	13 Dec. 1960	3 July 1962	17 Apr. 1964	Alex. Stephen & Sons Ltd., Govan

ZULU

| JAGUAR | LEOPARD | LYNX | PUMA |

Known as the "Leopard" class, these 1st Rate frigates of the diesel-powered anti-aircraft type were designed primarily for the protection of convoys against air attack, but it was officially stated that they were also intended to serve as destroyers for offensive operations. The 4.5-inch twin gun turrets, mountings and armament control are similar to those mounted in the large destroyers of the "Daring" class. Named after big cats, they are all welded, and the structural arrangements represented the latest in the development of modern technique, opportunity having been taken during construction to study the problems of rapid production of such ships in emergency. Officially listed as 'Type 41", they are fitted with stabilisers. The propelling machinery consists of Admiralty Standard Range I heavy oil engines coupled to the propeller shafting through hydraulic couplings and oil-operated reverse and reduction gear boxes. *Jaguar* is fitted with controllable pitch propellers. The ani-aircraft guns in all ships will be replaced by a "Seacat" surface-to-air guided missile quadruple launcher. *Lynx* was refitted with a main "mack", or combined mast-stack in 1963, *Puma* in 1964, and *Leopard* in 1964–66, followed by *Jaguar*.

Standard displacement	Full load displacement	Length	Beam	Draught
2,300 tons	2,520 tons	340 feet	40 feet	16 feet

Main guns	Anti-aircraft guns	Anti-submarine weapons	Guided weapons
4–4.5 inch	1–40 mm.	"Squid" triple-barrelled depth charge mortar	"Seacat" to be fitted in *Jaguar*

Propelling machinery	Brake horse power	Speed	Complement
8 A.S.R.1 diesels	12,380	25 knots	205

Name	No.	Begun	Launched	Completed	Builders
JAGUAR	F 37	2 Nov. 1953	30 July 1957	12 Dec. 1959	Wm. Denny & Bros. Ltd., Dumbarton
LEOPARD	F 14	25 Mar. 1953	23 May 1955	30 Sept. 1958	H.M. Dockyard, Portsmouth
LYNX	F 27	13 Aug. 1953	12 Jan. 1955	14 Mar. 1957	John Brown & Co. Ltd., Clydebank
PUMA	F 34	16 Nov. 1953	30 June 1954	24 Apr. 1957	Scotts' S.B. & Eng. Co. Ltd., Greenock

JAGUAR

CHICHESTER   LINCOLN   LLANDAFF   SALISBURY

The 1st Rate frigates of this aircraft direction type, known as the "Salisbury" class, were primarily designed for the direction of carrier-borne and shore-based aircraft, and they can be employed as ocean radar pickets. They were also intended as a type of destroyers in offensive operations. Their hull design, dimensions and propelling machinery are similar to those of the "Leopard" class anti-aircraft frigates, but they have only one 4.5-inch twin turret, mounted forward as in the "Whitby" class anti-submarine frigates. In 1962 *Salisbury* underwent extended refit, her after funnel inside a lattice mast replaced by a combined "mack" or combined mast-stack to support a much larger radar aerial. *Chichester* was similarly refitted in 1964 but with both fore and main "macks", *Llandaff* in 1966, followed by *Lincoln*. Officially listed as "Type 61", these ships have very highly developed electronic equipment. Their construction was all welded, and designed to be largely prefabricated in such a manner as to allow for rapid building in emergency. *Llandaff* has a gas turbine alternator. All ships of this class are named after cathedral cities. The ship allocated the name *Coventry* was in fact built as *Penelope* of the "Leander" class.

Standard displacement	Full load displacement	Length	Beam	Draught
2,170 tons	2,350 tons	340 feet	40 feet	15½ feet

Main guns	Anti-aircraft guns	Anti-submarine weapons	Guided weapons
2–4.5 inch	1–40 mm. and/or 2–20 mm	"Squid" triple-barrelled depth charge mortar	"Seacat" to be fitted

Propelling machinery	Brake horse power	Speed	Complement
8 A.S.R.1 diesels	12,380	25 knots	207

Name	No.	Begun	Launched	Completed	Builders
CHICHESTER	F 59	25 Jan. 1953	21 Apr. 1955	16 May 1957	Fairfield S.B. & Eng. Co. Ltd., Glasgow
LINCOLN	F 99	20 May 1955	6 Apr. 1959	7 July 1960	Fairfield S.B. & Eng. Co. Ltd., Glasgow
LLANDAFF	F 61	27 Aug. 1953	30 Nov. 1955	11 Apr. 1958	Hawthorn Leslie Ltd., Hebburn-on-Tyne
SALISBURY	F 32	23 Jan. 1952	25 June 1953	27 Feb. 1957	H.M. Dockyard, Devonport

CHICHESTER

BLACKWOOD	DUNDAS	GRAFTON	KEPPEL	MURRAY	PELLEW
DUNCAN	EXMOUTH	HARDY	MALCOLM	PALLISER	RUSSELL

2nd Rate frigates of anti-submarine "utility" type, known as the "Blackwood" class, of novel, very lightly armed type, as far as guns are concerned, designed mainly for submarine hunting and killing. Of comparatively simple construction. Designed in prefabricated sections. Their two "Limbo" ahead-projecting anti-submarine multiple mortars can each fire a pattern of large depth charges with great accuracy, the projectiles set to explode at any predetermined depth. These weapons can be trained over a wider arc than any previous type of anti-submarine mortars and have much greater and more accurate range. *Duncan*, fitted as squadron leader, *Malcolm*, *Palliser* and *Russell* formed the Royal Navy's Fishery Protection Squadron in 1958–59. All ships of this class are named after famous naval captains of the past, and are officially listed as "Type 14". In 1958–59 all ships had their hulls strengthened. In 1966–68 *Exmouth* was reconstructed and converted to all-gas turbine propulsion with one Olympus engine of 22,500 h.p. and two Proteus engines each of 3,250 h.p. but only one system or the other propels; they cannot be used together or for boost.

Standard displacement	Full load displacement	Length	Beam	Draught
1,180 tons	1,456 tons	310 feet	33 feet	15½ feet *max.*

Anti-aircraft guns	Torpedo tubes	Anti-submarine weapons	Complement
2–40 mm. (one removed)	(4–21 inch removed)	2 "Limbo" three-barrelled depth charge mortars	140

Propelling machinery	Shaft horse power	Boilers	Speed	Completed
Geared steam turbines	15,000	2 Babcock & Wilocx	28 knots	Dec. 1955 to Oct. 1958
(*Exmouth*: gas turbines)	(*Exmouth* 22,500)	(except *Exmouth*)		

Note: Of "Bay" class frigates, *Morecambe Bay* and *Mounts Bay* transferred to Portugal in 1961, *Porlock Bay* to Finland in 1962, and *Cardigan Bay* and *St. Brides Bay* were scrapped in 1962. Of "Loch" class frigates only *Loch Fada* and *Loch Killisport* remained in 1968. *Loch Insh* was transferred to Malaysia in 1964. *Loch Craggie, Loch More,* and *Loch Tralaig* were scrapped in 1963, *Loch Alvie* and *Loch Veyatie* in 1965, *Loch Ruthven* in 1966, followed by *Loch Fyne* and *Loch Lomond* (see particulars in 1960 Edition).

PELLEW

ZEST   WAKEFUL   VERULAM   GRENVILLE   ULSTER   TROUBRIDGE   RAPID
UNDAUNTED   RELENTLESS

These vessels, known as the "full conversion" class, and officially listed as "Type 15", represented the post-war British conception of fast anti-submarine frigates. Originally completed in 1942–4 as standard destroyers of the "Z", "W", "V", "U", "T" and "R" flotillas, in 1949–57 they underwent complete reconstruction and conversion involving stripping down to the hull, extending the forecastle deck aft, erecting fuller superstructure and mounting entirely new armament. There are various differences between them, especially in armament disposition and bridge structure. Australian and Canadian destroyers of the "Q", "V" and "Cr" flotillas were converted in a very similar manner. The Australian ships have the bridge a deck higher and the forward guns before the bridge; the Canadian ships have the forward guns on the forecastle deck level and mount 3-inch instead of 40-mm. guns. Tubes, where mounted, were fixed and intended for anti-submarine homing torpedoes, not the conventional type. *Wrangler* of this full conversion type was transferred to the South African Navy and renamed *Vrystaat* in 1956, *Roebuck*, *Ulysses*, *Undine* and *Vigilant* were scheduled for disposal in 1962, *Rocket* and *Virago* in 1963, *Urchin* and *Venus* in 1965, *Volage* (used as Harbour Training Ship for Royal Marines), *Whirlwind* and *Wizard* in 1966, *Urania* and *Ursa* in 1968.

	Standard displacement	Full load displacement	Length	Beam	Draught
"R" class:	2,200 tons	2,710 tons	358¼ feet	35⅔ feet	17 feet *max.*
Others:	2,240 tons	2,880 tons	362¾ feet	35⅔ feet	17 feet *max.*

Main guns	Anti-aircraft guns	Torpedo tubes	Anti-submarine weapons
2–4 inch	2–40 mm.	2 to 8, or none	2 "Squid" or 2 "Limbo" three-barrelled depth charge mortars

Propelling machinery	Shaft horse power	Boilers	Speed	Complement
Geared steam turbines	40,000	2 Admiralty 3-drum type	31.25 to 36·75 knots	180 to 195

Note: The five surviving "limited conversion" or "Type 16" fast anti-submarine frigates, *Orwell*, *Petard*, *Terpischore*, *Tumult* and *Tuscan*, were scrapped in 1965–66.

ZEST

6 "KOLA" CLASS   **50 "RIGA" CLASS**

The design of the "Kola" class of flush-decked, two-funnelled destroyer escorts or frigates appears to be a combination of that of the German "Elbing" type torpedo boat destroyers, with a similar hull form, and of the older Soviet frigates of the "Birds" class. The four 3.9 inch guns, which are similar to the main armament in the "Birds" class frigates are mounted as in the "Gordi" class destroyers. The "Kola" class were originally reported to number 12 units.

The very handsome and rakish-looking escort vessels or frigates of the "Riga" class are of the light destroyer or oceangoing torpedo boat type. They appear to be a lighter and less heavily armed but improved version of the "Kola" class destroyer escorts in design. The class was sub-divided into two types with different schemes of masting. The earlier group had a tied tripod foremast, while the later units have a substantial lattice foremast to support heavier radar aerials with a stepped back topmast. A number of this class have been transferred to other navies. The remainder have a uniform lattice scheme of masting.

Standard displacement	Full load displacement	Length	Beam	Draught
("Kola" class) 1,500 tons	2,000 tons	305 feet	32¾ feet	11½ feet
"Riga" class) 1,200 tons	1,600 tons	295 feet	31½ feet	11 feet

Main guns	Anti-aircraft guns	Torpedo tubes	Anti-submarine armament
("Kola" class) 4–3.9 inch	4–37 mm.	3–21 inch	Depth charge throwers and racks
("Riga" class) 3–3.9 inch	3–37 mm.	3–21 inch	4 depth charge projectors

Propelling machinery	Boilers	Shaft horse power	Speed	Complement
("Kola" class) Geared steam turbines	2	30,000	31 knots	190
("Riga" class) Geared steam turbines	2	25,000	28 knots	150

The older Soviet frigates, the Improved "Birds" class *Albatross, Chaika* and *Krechet*, and the "Birds" class, *Berkut, Gryf, Kondor, Korshun, Oryol, Voron* and *Yastreb*, were discarded in 1964–69

"KOLA" Class

"RIGA" Class

AMIRAL CHARNER
BALNY
COMMANDANT BORY
COMMANDANT BOURDAIS
COMMANDANT RIVIERE
DOUDART DE LA GREE
ENSEIGNE DE VAISSEAU HENRY
PROTET
VICTOR SCHOELCHER

These vessels of the "Commandant Rivière" class are of a new dual purpose type of sturdy and powerful appearance. First classed as *Escorteurs d'Union Francaise* (French overseas escorts) replacing the former colonial sloops, but officially re-rated as *Avisos Escorteurs* (sloop escorts) in 1959. Designed to serve as *avisos* or sloops in peacetime and anti-submarine frigates in wartime. Their main guns are of new automatic anti-aircraft design, and the large quadruple mortar is for both anti-submarine and anti-shore use. A light helicopter can land aft, and a commando unit of 80 men can be carried in addition to the ship's company. *Balny* and *Commandant Bory* have Sigma free piston generators and gas turbines, while the others have four SEMT-Pielstick diesels coupled two by two on two shafts. All nine ships were built in Lorient Naval Dockyard and completed for active service in 1962, 1968, 1964, 1963, 1962, 1963, 1965, 1964 and 1962, respectively, in alphabetical order of names above. *Commandant Rivière*, the name-ship of the class, and the prototype, started assembly on the slip in Nov. 1956 and was commissioned to run sea trials in Apr. 1959. *Commandant Bourdais* was commissioned as a fishery protection ship in Mar. 1963. *Victor Schoelcher* acts as training ship.

Standard displacement	*Full load displacement*	*Length*	*Beam*	*Draught*
1,750 tons	2,230 tons	338 feet	$37\frac{3}{4}$ feet	$14\frac{1}{4}$ feet

Main guns	*Secondary guns*	*Torpedo tubes*	*Anti-submarine weapons*
3–3.9 inch dual purpose (2 in Balny)	2–30 mm. anti-aircraft	6–21 inch	1–12 inch quadruple mortar

Propelling machinery	*Brake horse power*	*Speed*	*Complement*
4 SEMT-Pielstick diesels (seven ships) Sigma generators and gas turbines (*B., C.B.*)	14,000 to 16,200	25 to 26.5 knots	214 to 220

DOUDART DE LA GREE

LE BORDELAIS	L'AGENAIS	LE BEARNAIS	LE CHAMPENOIS	LE PICARD
LE BOULONNAIS	L'ALSACIEN	LE BOURGUIGNON	LE GASCON	LE PROVENCAL
LE BRESTOIS	LE BASQUE	LE BRETON	LE LORRAIN	LE SAVOYARD
LE CORSE			LE NORMAND	LE VENDEEN

The first four of these fast frigates, *Le Bordelais*, *Le Boulonnais*, *Le Brestois* and *Le Corse*, constituting the "E 50 Type" or "Le Corse" class, completed in 1955–6, were the first French escorts built since the Second World War. In design they resemble that of the United States destroyer escorts of the "Dealey" class. Intended as seagoing convoy escort vessels with a large radius of action, they were planned as *Escorteurs Rapides Anti-Sousmarins*, but re-rated *Escorteurs de Deuxiéme Classe* in 1951, *Escorteurs* in 1953, and *Escorteurs Rapides* in 1955. The fourteen later vessels known as the "E 52a Type" or "Le Normand" class, completed in 1956–9, have similar hull and machinery but are easily distinguished in that they have the anti-submarine tubes aft and the heavy Hedgehog or anti-submarine howitzer forward, while the "E 50" type have the ASM torpedo tubes forward. *L'Agenais*, *L'Alsacien*, *Le Béarnais*, *Le Provencal* and *Le Vendeen* have a 12-inch quadruple mortar in place of the sextuple Bofors howitzer and only four 57-mm. anti-aircraft guns. *L'Alsacien*, *Le Bordelais*, *Le Provencal* and *Le Vendeen* have the Strombos-Valensi modified funnel cap. Owing to financial difficulties construction of the two frigates of the "E 52b" type, planned under the 1957 naval estimates, was abandoned.

Standard displacement	Full load displacement	Length	Beam	Draught
1,290 to 1,295 tons	1,680 to 1,795 tons	338 feet	33¾ feet	13½ feet *max.*

Main guns	Secondary guns	Torpedo tubes	Anti-submarine weapons	
4 or 6–57 mm. AA.	2–20 mm. AA.	12–21.7 inch	12 inch quadruple mortar or sextuple howitzer	

Propelling machinery	Shaft horse power	Boilers	Speed	Complement
Geared steam turbines	20,000	2	27 to 28 knots	174 to 198

LE BRETON

ALPINO	*BERSAGLIERE*	CARABINIERE	*GRANATIERE*

Racy looking ships with rake and flare and generally presenting a handsome and powerful appearance. *Alpino* and *Carabiniere*, initially to have been named *Circe* and *Climene*, respectively, were provided for under the 1959–60 new construction programme, but the original "Circe" class project was modified in 1962 in respect of both propelling machinery and armament, and the names were changed in June 1965. The new design is understood to be an improved version of that of the "Centaur" class combined with that of the "Bergamini" class. They have similar basic characteristics but a heavier displacement and increased engine power. Two other ships of the same type, originally to have been named *Perseo* and *Polluce*, but later allocated the names *Bersagliere* and *Granatiere*, were provided for under the 1960–61 new construction programme but they were suspended for the time being owing to financial considerations.

Standard displacement	Full load displacement	Length	Beam	Draught
2,419 tons	2,689 tons	371⅔ feet	43 feet	12⅔ feet

Guns	Torpedo tubes	Anti-submarine weapons	Aircraft
6–3 inch dual purpose (single)	6–12 inch (2 triple)	1 single barrel D.C. mortar	2 A/B 204 B ASW helicopters

Propelling machinery	Shaft horse power	Speed	Complement
4 diesels	16,800	22 knots (diesels)	254
2 gas turbines	15,000	28 knots (combined)	

Name	No.	Begun	Launched	Completed	Builders
ALPINO	F 580	27 Feb. 1963	10 June 1967	14 Jan. 1968	Cantiere Navali del Tirreno, Riva Trigoso
CARABINIERE	F 581	9 Jan. 1965	30 Sept. 1967	30 Apr. 1968	Cantiere Navali del Terreno, Riva Trigoso

ALPINO

CANOPO	CASTORE	CENTAURO	CIGNO

These ships, known as the "Centauro" class, have special anti-submarine and medium anti-aircraft armament. *Cigno* and *Castore* were built to Italian plans and specifications under the United States off-shore programme for the Italian Navy. All four ships have U.S. sonar gear. Although officially rated as frigates they are light destroyers or destroyer escorts (*Cigno* and *Castore* originally had DE numbers—1020 and 1021, respectively) and all four had D numbers until 1960 when they were changed to F numbers. The four 3-inch guns formerly mounted were in twin gunhouses of a new type with the two barrels in the vertical plane, one superfiring over the other. This two-barrelled 76/62 calibre gun was Italian designed and built by Ansaldo, and its rate of fire was 80 rounds per minute with 3,200 feet per second muzzle velocity. But in 1966–67 *Castore* was converted to the armament shown below and her three sisters are being similarly refitted.

Standard displacement	Full load displacement	Length	Beam	Draught
1,807 tons	2,196 tons	338 feet	39½ feet	12⅝ feet

Main and anti-aircraft guns	Torpedo tubes	Anti-submarine armament
3–3 inch (single)	6 launchers (2 triple)	1 triple-barrelled long range depth charge mortar

Propelling machinery	Shaft horse power	Boilers	Speed	Complement
Geared steam turbines	22,000	2 Foster Wheeler	26 knots	255

Name	Pennant No.	Begun	Launched	Completed	Builders
CANOPO	F552 (ex-D570)	15 May 1952	20 Feb. 1955	1 Apr. 1958	Cantieri Navali di Taranto
CENTAURO	F554 (ex-D571)	31 May 1952	4 Apr. 1954	5 May 1957	Ansaldo, Leghorn
CIGNO	F555 (ex-D572)	10 Feb. 1954	20 Mar. 1955	7 Mar. 1957	Cantieri Navali di Taranto
CASTORE	F553 (ex-D573)	14 Mar. 1955	8 July 1956	14 July 1957	Cantieri Navali di Taranto

Note: Italy also has three former U.S. "Bostwick" class destroyer escorts, *Aldebaran, Altair* and *Andromeda*, rated as frigates.

CASTORE

CARLO BERGAMINI   CARLO MARGOTTINI   LUIGI RIZZO   VIRGINIO FASAN

These unusual looking vessels are light frigates of a new type with diesel instead of steam propulsion. Originally they were rated as *Corvette Veloci tipo II* (Fast Corvettes, "CV 2" Type), but their plans underwent many amendments since they were first projected, and when they started trials in 1961 they were very different ships from those initially envisaged. Their armament and superstructure rises in a shallow pyramid from forecastle and quarter deck to a "mack" or combination mast-stack at the summit, abaft which is a small hangar for the helicopter operating from the flight apron on the shelter deck. Despite their unconventional layout they contrive a quite symmetrical appearance with a racy profile. Each of the 62-calibre fully automatic guns comprising the main armament has a rate of fire of 57 rounds per minute; and the single barrelled long range depth charge mortar has a range of over 1,000 yards. All the ships are fitted with Denny-Brown stabilisers.

Standard displacement	Full load displacement	Length	Beam	Draught
1,410 tons	1,650 tons	308¼ feet	37¼ feet	10⅓ feet

Guns	Torpedo tubes	Anti-submarine weapons	Aircraft
3–3 inch (single)	6 (two triple)	1 single-barrelled automatic long range depth charge mortar	light helicopter

Propelling machinery	Brake horse power	Speed	Complement
4 Tosi diesels (*C. Bergamini* and *L. Rizzo*) 4 Fiat diesels (*C. Margottini* and *V. Fasan*)	15,000	26 knots	160

Name	No.	Begun	Launched	Completed	Builders
CARLO BERGAMINI	F 593	16 May 1957	16 June 1960	23 June 1962	San Marco, C.R.D.A., Trieste
CARLO MARGOTTINI	F 595	26 May 1957	12 June 1960	5 May 1962	Navalmeccanica, Castellammare
LUIGI RIZZO	F 596	26 May 1957	6 Mar. 1960	15 Dec. 1961	Navalmeccanica, Castellammare
VIRGINIO FASAN	F 594	6 Mar. 1960	9 Oct. 1960	10 Oct. 1962	Navalmeccanica, Castellammare

LUIGI RIZZO

EVERTSEN   ISAAC SWEERS   TJERK HIDDES   VAN GALEN   VAN NES   VAN SPEIJK

These general purpose frigates, projected as a class of six units, are basically similar to the improved Type 12 frigates of the first rate anti-submarine versatile group in the Royal Navy known as the "Leander" class. To avoid delay and to get them into service with the Royal Netherlands Navy as soon as possible these new frigates were fitted with equipment available at short notice instead of that still in the development stage, and as far as practicable equipment of Netherlands manufacture was installed, a course which resulted in a number of changes in the ships' superstructure. Four ships were ordered in 1962 and the other two later. Although in general they are based on the design of the highly successful British "Leander" class frigates they have small modifications in accordance with the requirements of the Royal Netherlands Navy. Known as the "Van Speijk" class, they were built as replacements for the six old and small frigates of the "Van Amstel" class, formerly United States destroyer escorts of the "Bostwick" class built in 1943.

Standard displacement	Full load displacement	Length	Beam	Draught
2,200 tons	2,850 tons	372 feet	41 feet	18 feet

Guided weapons	Guns	Anti-submarine weapons	Aircraft
2 quadruple launchers for "Seacat" missiles	2–4.5 inch	1 3-barrel "Limbo" mortar	helicopter

Propelling machinery	Shaft horse power	Boilers	Speed	Complement
Geared steam turbines	30,000	2 Babcock & Wilcox	28½ knots	254

Name	Begun	Launched	Completed	Builders
EVERTSEN	5 May 1965	18 June 1966	1968	Koninklijke Maatschappij De Schelde, Flushing
ISAAC SWEERS	5 May 1965	10 Mar. 1967	1969	Nederlandse Dok en Scheepsbouw Mij., Amsterdam
TJERK HIDDES	1 June 1964	17 Dec. 1965	1967	Nederlandse Dok en Scheepsbouw Mij., Amsterdam
VAN GALEN	25 July 1963	19 June 1965	1967	Koninklijke Maatschappij De Schelde, Flushing
VAN NES	25 July 1963	26 Mar. 1966	1968	Koninklijke Maatschappij De Schelde, Flushing
VAN SPEIJK	1 Oct. 1963	5 Mar. 1965	1967	Nederlandse Dok en Scheepsbouw Mij., Amsterdam

VAN SPEIJK

AUGSBURG   BRAUNSCHWEIG   EMDEN   KARLSRUHE   KÖLN   LÜBECK

Köln was the prototype and name-ship of a novel class of fast anti-submarine frigates or escort vessels ordered in March 1957 and all built by the same shipyard, H. C. Stülcken Sohn, Hamburg, for the *Bundesmarine*. Of both handsome and racy appearance, their construction is more reminiscent of that of torpedo boat destroyers than of frigates, and their evenly distributed armament gives them a symmetrical layout. Their propelling machinery consists of a combined diesel and gas turbine plant comprising four 16-cylinder M.A.N. diesels aggregating 12,000 brake horse power coupled to two Brown Boveri gas turbines developing 26,000 horse power, the two shafts fitted with variable pitch propellers giving them a total shaft horse power equal to a trial speed of 32 knots. Formerly designated *Geleitboote*, but now rated as *Fregatten*, they are the first frigates built for the Federal German Navy. All are named after towns of West Germany.

(The Federal German Navy also has two former British frigates, *Scharnhorst* (ex-H.M.S. *Mermaid*) of the "Black Swan" class and *Gneisenau* (ex-H.M.S. *Oakley*) of the "Hunt" class. *Brommy* (ex-*Eggesford*), *Graf Spee* (ex-*Flamingo*), *Hipper* (ex-*Actaeon*), *Raule* (ex-*Albrighton*) and *Scheer* (ex-*Hart*) were decommissioned in 1964–68 for scrap).

Standard displacement	*Full load displacement*	*Length*	*Beam*	*Draught*
2,100 tons	2,550 tons	361 feet	36¼ feet	12 feet

Main guns	*Anti-aircraft guns*	*Anti-submarine weapons*	*Torpedo tubes*
2–3.9 inch (100 mm.) (single)	6–40 mm. (2 twin, 2 single)	2 four-barrelled depth charge mortars (Bofors rocket launchers)	2 for ASW torpedoes

Propelling machinery	*Shaft horse power*	*Speed*	*Complement*
Combined diesels and gas turbines	38,000	30 knots	210

Name	*No.*	*Launched*	*Completed*	*Name*	*No.*	*Launched*	*Completed*
AUGSBURG	F 222	15 Aug. 1959	7 Apr. 1962	KARLSRUHE	F 223	24 Oct. 1959	15 Dec. 1962
BRAUNSCHWEIG	F 225	3 Feb. 1962	16 June 1964	KÖLN	F 220	6 Dec. 1958	15 Apr. 1961
EMDEN	F 221	21 Mar. 1959	24 Oct. 1961	LÜBECK	F 224	23 July 1960	6 July 1963

KÖLN

ISUZU	MOGAMI	IKAZUCHI	AKEBONO
KITAKAMI	OHI	INAZUMA	

The four vessels of the "Mogami" or "River" class were frigates or destroyer escorts of new design. *Isuzu* and *Mogami* were completed in 1961, *Kitakami* and *Ohi* in 1964. All new frigates of the DE type were named after rivers, like the old light cruisers. This naming system applied in 1960.

The two units of the "Ikazuchi" or "Thunder" class are diesel powered escort vessels, and unlike the third vessel built under the initial post-war construction programme, the steam turbine propelled *Akebono*, which has two funnels, have only one funnel. Both were completed in 1956.

Akebono (meaning "Dawn"), was the first destroyer escort laid down since the end of the Second World War for the Japanese Maritime Self-Defence Force. Also completed in 1956, she looks more like a destroyer than her half-sisters *Ikazuchi* and *Inazuma*.

(Japan also has 9 other vessels listed under the frigate category: *Wakaba*, an escort destroyer of the former Imperial Japanese Navy, sunk soon after she was completed in 1945, but subsequently raised and reconstructed in 1956 and now rated as a radar experimental ship; *Ashi* and *Hatsuhi*, ex-U.S. destroyer escorts of the "Bostwick" class; and *Kaya, Keyaki, Kiri, Nire, Shii, Sugi,* all ex-U.S. patrol frigates of the "Tacoma" class.)

Standard displacement	*Full load displacement*	*Length*	*Beam*	*Draught*
"Mogami" class: 1,490 tons	1,700 tons	308½ feet	34¼ feet	11½ feet
"Ikazuchi" class: 1,070 tons	1,300 tons	288⅔ feet	28½ feet	10¼ feet
Akebono: 1,060 tons	1,350 tons	295 feet	28½ feet	11 feet

Main and anti-aircraft guns	*Torpedo tubes, launchers*	*Anti-submarine weapons*
4–3 inch AA. (two twin)	4–21 inch (quad), 2 triple homing	1 rocket launcher, 1 d.c.t., 1 d.c.r.
2–3 inch d.p.; 2–40 mm. AA.		1 Hedgehog, 8 K-guns, 2 D.C. racks
2–3 inch dual purpose (single)		1 Hedgehog, 4 K-guns, 2 D.C. racks

Propelling machinery	*Shaft horse power*	*Boilers*	*Speed*	*Complement*
Diesel engines	16,000		26 knots	180
Diesel engines	12,000		25 knots	160
Geared steam turbines	18,000	2 Foster Wheeler	28 knots	190

MOGAMI

"Annapolis" Class	"Mackenzie" Class	"Restigouche" Class		"St. Laurent" Class	
ANNAPOLIS	MACKENZIE	CHAUDIERE	RESTIGOUCHE	ASSINIBOINE	SAGUENAY
NIPIGON	QU'APPELLE	COLUMBIA	ST. CROIX	FRASER	ST. LAURENT
	SASKATCHEWAN	GATINEAU	TERRA NOVA	MARGAREE	SKEENA
	YUKON	KOOTENAY		OTTAWA	

The "St. Laurent" class were officially classed as major warships and as such were the first to be designed completely in Canada. These anti-submarine destroyer escorts or fast frigates were built primarily for the detection and destruction of modern submarines, and in evolving their design much assistance was received from the Royal Navy and the United States Navy. In function the vessels supersede the frigates of the Second World War, and their design was worked out so that in emergency they could be produced rapidly and in quantity. The design provided for flush deck, low bridge, considerable use of aluminium instead of steel for the superstructure, fittings and furniture, and compartmented hull. The "Restigouche" class were basically similar to the "St. Laurent" class, but there was a considerable difference in the bridge structure, which is higher at the break of the forecastle and drops down to a new breakwater deck on which the new British 3 inch, 70 calibre twin gun in enclosed turret is mounted and over which it has better vision. There is also a difference in the shelter deck superstructure and fittings abaft the funnel, wing platforms on the foremast, director and look-out wings abaft the bridge, and improved sonar gear. New features of the "Mackenzie" class include improved habitability reduced complement, and air conditioning, and extension of the pre-wetting system (to counter radio-active fallout) to cover the entire exposed area of the ship. The last two ships of the "Mackenzie" class, *Annapolis* and *Nipigon*, which incorporate variable depth sonar, cutaway stern, and helicopter platform, were separated into a new class. All seven ships of the "St. Laurent" class have been similarly reconstructed with helo flight apron VDS, and twin athwartships funnels stepped to permit forward extension of the hangar.

	Standard displacement	Full load displacement	Length	Beam	Draught
"St. L." class	2,263 tons	2,800 tons	366 feet	42 feet	$13\frac{1}{4}$ feet
"Rest" class	2,366 tons	2,900 tons	371 feet	42 feet	$13\frac{1}{4}$ feet

Anti-submarine weapons	Anti-aircraft guns	Torpedoes	Helicopter
1 or 2 "Limbo" three-barrelled depth charge mortars	2 or 4-3 inch (twin)	Homing	*Ann.* and *St. L.* cl.

Propelling machinery	Shaft horse power	Boilers	Speed	Complement
Geared steam turbines	30,000	2 water tube	$28\frac{1}{4}$ knots	246 to 250

Completed:—"St. Laurent" class 1955–57; "Restigouche" class 1958–59; "Mackenzie" class 1962–63; "Annapolis" class 1964.

NIPIGON

MACKENZIE

SKEENA

BADGER	FRANCIS HAMMOND	KNOX	MEYERCORD	ROARK
BLAKELY	GRAY	LANG	PATTERSON	TRIPPE
CONNOLE	HAROLD E. HOLT	LOCKWOOD	RATHBURNE	VREELAND
DOWNES	HEPBURN	MARVIN SHIELDS	REASONER	WHIPPLE
				W. S. SIMS

The fifty escort ships of the "Knox" class built and building are the numerically largest group of vessels of the destroyer type constructed to the same design by any navy since the end of the Second World War, and to a considerable extent they will compensate for the large number of small and obsolescent destroyers and destroyer escorts built upwards of 25 years ago which are destined for the shipbreakers shortly. Designated DE 1052 to DE 1101, the "Knox" class are similar in design to that of the earlier 'Brooke" and "Garcia" classes but are somewhat larger. Although they were designed to operate drone anti-submarine warfare helicopters it is possible that they will carry manned light airborne ASW vehicles (LAAVs) in the 1970s. The 21 ships named at the time of writing, see above, were launched in 1966 to 1969. DE 1101 will have a gas turbine power plant.

Standard displacement	Full load displacement	Length	Beam	Draught
3,077 tons	4,100 tons	438 feet	47 feet	25 feet

Guided weapons	Guns	Anti-submarine armament
BPDMS launcher for Sparrow III missiles	1–5 inch dual purpose	1 ASROC 8-tube launcher, 2 triple torpedo launchers, 2 fixed torpedo tubes, 2 DASH (drone anti-submarine helicopters)

Propelling machinery	Shaft horse power	Boilers	Speed	Complement
1 geared steam turbine	35,000	2 high pressure	27 knots	245

KNOX

"Brooke" Class		"Garcia" Class		
BROOKE	RICHARD L. PAGE	ALBERT DAVID	EDWARD McDONNELL	O'CALLAHAN
JULIUS A. FURER	SCHOFIELD	BRADLEY	GARCIA	SAMPLE
RAMSAY	TALBOT	BRUMBY	KOELSCH	VOGE
		DAVIDSON		

These fleet escort ships were designed primarily for anti-submarine warfare, but the six vessels of the "Brooke" class, *Brooke*, *Julius A. Furer*, *Ramsay*, *Richard L. Page*, *Schofield* and *Talbot*, had an anti-aircraft missile system installed instead of a second 5 inch gun. Although they are larger than many destroyers they are listed under the escort ship category on account of their single screw and comparatively moderate speed. In design they are an expansion of that of the "Bronstein" class escort ships, the prototype pair of larger destroyer escorts. All the ships of the group have an advanced pressure fired steam generating plant which develops seventy per cent more power than previous steam plants of the same size and weight, yet needs fewer marine engineering personnel to operate the machinery. The ships have a central "mack", or combined mast and stack, flush deck, acutely raked stem, bow anchor, and stabilising fins. The six vessels of the "Brooke" class are designated DEGs (DEG 1 to 6) while the ten ships of the "Garcia" class are designated DEs (DE 1040, 1041, 1043, 1044, 1045 and 1047 to 1051). All were completed between 1964 and 1968. The escort research ship **GLOVER**, AGDE 1, is practically identical to the "Brooke" class above the waterline and has a full combat capability.

	Standard displacement	Full load displacement	Length	Beam	Draught
"Brooke" class:	2,643 tons	3,426 tons	414½ feet	44 feet	24 feet
"Garcia" class:	2.624 tons	3.403 tons	414½ feet	44 feet	24 feet

	Guided weapons	Guns	Complement
"Brooke" class:	1 single launcher for "Tartar" surface-to-air missiles	1–5 inch dual purpose	241
"Garcia" class:		2–5 inch dual purpose	245

	Propelling machinery	Shaft horse power	Boilers	Speed	Anti-submarine weapons
Both classes:	1 geared turbine	35.000	2	27 knots	1 ASROC 8-tube launcher. 2 triple torpedo launchers. 2 fixed torpedo tubes (stern). 2 DASH helicopters

BROOKE

GARCIA

GLOVER

McCLOY

CHARLES BERRY

BRONSTEIN	CHARLES BERRY	BAUER	EVANS	JOHN WILLIS
McCLOY	CLAUD JONES	BRIDGET	HAMMERBERG	JOSEPH K. TAUSSIG
	JOHN R. PERRY	COURTNEY	HARTLEY	LESTER
	McMORRIS	CROMWELL	HOOPER	VAN VOORHIS
		DEALEY		

Intended for fast convoy protection, the "Dealey" group were designed for mass production in event of war and are contemporary with British 2nd Rate anti-submarine frigates. The distinctive type letter symbol "DE", denoting the category to which these ships belong, stands for "Destroyer Escort", but in the United States official list of classifications of naval vessels they are grouped under the generic heading of "Patrol Ships" with the specific sub-category of "Escort Ships". However, they approximate to the smaller ships of the frigate category in British and other navies. With a single engine-room, single screw, twin rudders and aluminium superstructure, saving forty per cent in weight, they are lavishly equipped with electronic gear. *Charles Berry, Claud Jones, John R. Perry* and *McMorris* ("Claud Jones" class) are of different type, being propelled by diesels instead of turbines, as in *Bronstein* and *McCloy* and the thirteen ships of the "Dealey" group.

	Standard displacement	Full load displacement	Length	Beam	Draught
"Dealey" group:	1,450 tons	1.914 tons	314½ feet	36¾ feet	13¾ feet
"Claud Jones" class:	1,450 tons	1.750 tons	312 feet	37 feet	18 feet
Bronstein. McCloy:	1,890 tons	2.650 tons	371½ feet	40½ feet	23 feet

	Guns	Anti-submarine weapons	Complement	Completed
"Dealey" group:	2 or 4–3 inch dual purpose	1 launcher	149 to 170	1954–1958
"Claud Jones" class:	2–3 inch dual purpose	2 launchers	175	1959–1960
Bronstein. McCloy:	3–3 inch dual purpose	3 launchers	220	1963

	Propelling machinery	Shaft horse power	Boilers	Speed
'Dealey" group:	1 set De Laval geared turbines	20.000	2 Foster-Wheeler	25 knots
"Claud Jones" class:	4 Fairbanks Morse diesels	12.000		21 knots
Bronstein, McCloy:	1 set geared turbines	23,000	2 Foster-Wheeler	26 knots

DEALEY

"Rudderow" Class

CHARLES H. KIMME
COATES
DE LONG
DAY
EUGENE E. ELMORE
HODGES
JOBB
LESLIE L. B. KNOX
LOUGH
McNULTY
METIVIER
PARLE
RILEY
RUDDEROW
THOMAS F. NICKEL
TINSMAN

"John C. Butler" Class

ABERCROMBIE
ALBERT T. HARRIS
ALVIN C. COCKERELL
BIVIN
CHARLES E. BRANNON
CHESTER T. O'BRIEN
CONKLIN
CORBESIER
DENNIS
DOYLE C. BARNES
DUFILHO

EDMONDS
EDWARD H. ALLEN
EDWIN A. HOWARD
FRENCH
GENTRY
GEORGE E. DAVIS
GILLIGAN
GOSS
GRADY
HANNA
HOWARD F. CLARK
JACCARD
JACK MILLER
JOHN C. BUTLER
JOHN L. WILLIAMSON
JOHNNIE HUTCHINS
JOSEPH E. CONNOLLY
KENDAL C. CAMPBELL
KENNETH M. WILLETT
KEY
LA PRADE
LAWRENCE C. TAYLOR
LE RAY WILSON
LELAND E. THOMAS
LLOYD E. ACREE
MACK
MELVIN R. NAWMAN
McGINTY
O'FLAHERTY
OLIVER MITCHELL

OSBERG
PRATT
PRESLEY
RAYMOND
RICHARD M. ROWELL
RICHARD S. BULL
RICHARD W. SUESENS
RIZZI
ROBERT F. KELLER
ROLF
ROMBACH
SILVERSTEIN
STAFFORD
TABBERER
TWEEDY
VANDIVIER
WAGNER
WALTER C. WANN
WALTON
WILLIAM SEIVERLING
WILLIAMS

"Buckley" Class

ALEXANDER J. LUKE
BUCKLEY
COOLBAUGH
CRONIN
DAMON M. CUMMINGS
DARBY
EICHENBERGER

FIEBERLING
FRANCIS M. ROBINSON
FRYBARGER
GENDREAU
GEORGE
GILLETTE
GUNASON
HENRY R. KENYON
HOLTON
JACK W. WILKE
JAMES E. CRAIG
J. DOUGLAS BLACKWOOD
LOESER
MAJOR
MANNING
MARSH
OSMUS
OTTER
PAUL G. BAKER
RABY
REUBE
ROBER
SPANGLER
THOMASON
VAMMEN
VARIAN
WEEDEN
WHITEHURST
WILLIAM C. COLE
WISEMAN

Three very similar types of escort vessels, the "Buckley" class forming the link between the two later types and the original "Edsall" and "Bostwick" classes later described. The "Buckley" class have tall funnels, whilst the others have short. Fifteen of the "Buckley" class mount two 5-inch guns, the others having three 3-inch as in the "Edsall" type. Ninety-two of the "Buckley" and "Rudderow" classes were converted into fast transports and nine units were converted into radar picket escort vessels (DER). All approximate to the British war-built frigate category, except that they are faster. Of the "Rudderow" class, *Holt* was transferred to South Korea in 1963, and *Daniel A. Joy*, *George A. Johnson* and *Peiffer* were strucken from the list in 1965–66. Of the "John C. Butler" class, *Formoe* and *McCoy Reynolds* were transferred to Portugal in 1957, and *Cecil J. Doyle*, *Cross*, *Douglas A. Munro*, *Haas*, *Heyliger*, *Jesse Rutherford*, *Lewis*, *Maurice J. Manuel*, *Naifeh*, *Robert Brazier*, *Strauss*, *Thaddeus Parker*, *Traw*, *Ulvert M. Moore* and *Woodson* were stricken in 1965–68. Of the "Buckley" class, *Ahrens*, *Borum*, *Currier*, *Durik*, *Earl V. Johnson*, *Fogg*, *Foreman*, *Foss*, *Fowler*, *Greenwood*, *Harmon*, *Jenks*, *Lovelace*, *Maloy*, *Neuendorf*, *Scott*, *Scroggis*, *Spandenburg*, *William T. Powell* and *Willmarth* were stricken in 1965–67.

Standard displacement	Full load displacement	Length	Beam	Draught
1,350 to 1,450 tons	2,100 to 2,230 tons	306 feet	37 feet	11 to 14 feet

Main guns	Anti-aircraft armament	Anti-submarine weapons	Complement
2–5 inch or 2 or 3–3 inch	2 to 8–40 mm	Hedgehogs, depth charge throwers	180 to 190

Propelling machinery	Shaft horse power	Boilers	Speed	Completed
Geared steam turbines	12,000	2	23 to 24 knots	1943-45

DE LONG
"Rudderow" Class

TWEEDY
"John C. Butler" Class

VANDIVIER
Converted "John C. Butler" Class

VAMMEN
"Buckley" Class

"Edsall" Class

	HURST	PETTIT	WILHOITE
	HUSE	POOLE	WILLIS
BLAIR	INCH	POPE	
BRISTER	JACOB JONES	PRICE	**"Bostwick" Class**
CALCATERRA	JANSSEN	PRIDE	ACREE
CAMP	JOYCE	RAMSDEN	COFFMAN
CHAMBERS	J. R. Y. BLAKELY	RHODES	COONER
CHATELAIN	KEITH	RICHEY	EARL K. OLSEN
COCKRILL	KIRKPATRICK	RICKETTS	HILBERT
DALE W. PETERSEN	KOINER	ROY O. HALE	KYNNE
DANIEL	KRETCHMER	SAVAGE	LAMONS
DOUGLAS L. HOWARD	LANCING	SLOAT	LEVY
DURANT	LOWE	SNOWDEN	McCLELLAND
EDSALL	MARCHAND	STANTON	McCONNELL
FALGOUT	MENGES	STEWART	NEAL A. SCOTT
FARQUHAR	MERRIL	STOCKDALE	OSTERHAUS
FINCH	MILLS	STRICKLAND	OSWALD
FORSTER	MOORE	STURTEVANT	PARKS
HAMMAN	MOSLEY	SWASEY	ROBERTS
HAVERFIELD	NEUNZER	SWENNING	SNYDER
HERBERT C. JONES	NEWELL	THOMAS J. GARY	STRAUB
HILL	O'REILLY	TOMICH	TILLS
HISSEM	OTTERSTETTER	VANCE	TRUMPETER
HOWARD D. CROW	PETERSEN		

These two classes represent the original Destroyer Escort design developed for escort duties with convoys and task forces. Ships of these classes were transferred to the Brazilian, Chinese Nationalist (Taiwan), French, Greek, Italian, Japanese, Netherlands, Peruvian, Philippine, South Korean, Thai and Uruguayan navies. Several units also served with the U.S. Coast Guard. Distinguishable from the later types by their tall funnels and 3-inch mounts in gun pits, these vessels could be confused with the 3-inch gunned ships of the "Buckley" class. Diesel or diesel-electric drive with a somewhat lower speed than the later types. Thirty-four units of the "Edsall" class were converted into radar picket escort vessels (DER). Ten ships of the "Edsall" class were stricken in 1965–67: *Brough, Fessenden, Flaherty, Frost, Harweson, J. Richard Ward, Martin H. Ray, Pillsbury, Robert E. Peary* and *Sellstrom.*

	Standard displacement	Full load displacement	Length	Beam	Draught
"Bostwick" class:	1,240 tons	1,900 tons	306 feet	37 feet	14 feet
"Edsall" class:	1,200 tons (1,590 tons DER)	1,850 tons	306 feet	37 feet	11 feet (14 DER)

	Main guns	Anti-aircraft guns	Torpedo tubes	Anti-submarine weapons
"Bostwick" class:	3–3 inch	2–40 mm.	Removed	Hedgehog and depth charges
"Edsall" class:	3–3 inch (2–3 inch in DER)	Up to 8–40 mm.	2 triple in some	Hedgehog and racks in DER

	Propelling machinery	Brake horse power	Speed	Complement	Completed
"Bostwick" class:	Diesel-electric	6,000	20 knots	150	1943–44
"Edsall" class:	Diesel	6,000	21 knots	149 (169 in DER)	1943–44

Note: Vandivier and *Wagner,* originally of the "John C. Butler" class, were completed as Radar Picket Escort Vessels (DER). *Alexander J. Luke, Buckley, Fogg, Reuben, James, Robert I. Payne, Spangenburg* and *William T. Powell* of the "Buckley" class, and the following vessels of the "Edsall" class were converted to Radar Picket Escort Vessels (DER):—
Blair, Brister, Calcaterra, Camp, Chambers, Durant, Falgout, Fessenden, Finch, Forster, Harweson, Haverfield, Hissem, Joyce, Kirkpatrick, Koiner, Kretchmer, Lancing, Lowe, Mills, Newell, Otterstetter, Pillsbury, Price, Ramsden, Rhodes, Roy O. Hale, Savage, Sellstrom, Strickland, Sturtevant, Thomas J. Gary, Vance and *Wilhoite.*

Of the "Bostwick" class, *Muir* and *Sutton* were transferred to the South Korean Navy in 1956, *Hemminger* was transferred to the Royal Thai Navy in 1959, and *Booth* to the Philippine Navy in 1968. *Carroll* and *Micka* were stricken in 1965.

PETERSEN
"Edsall" Class

EARL K. OLSEN
"Bostwick" Class

INDEX

Junon 53
Jupiter 126

Kalinin 68
Kalk 106
Kamehameha 40
Karlsruhe 14₁
Kashin *class* 107
Kearney 106
Kearsarge 16
Keith 153
Kendal C. Campbell 150
Kenneth D. Bailey 101
Kenneth M. Willett 150
Kent 79
Keppler 98
Kersaint 113
Key 150
Kidd 103
Kikuzki 118
Kildin *class* 109
Kiliç Ali Pasa 122
King 84
Kirkpatrick 153
Kirov 68
Kitakami 142
Kitty Hawk 14
Knapp 103
Knox 145
Koelsch 146
Koiner 153
Kola *class* 134
Köln 141
Komsomolets 67
Kootenay 143
Kotlin *class* 111
Kotlin Sam *class* 109, 110
Kresta *class* 87
Kretchmer 153
Krupny *class* 108
Kuibyshev 67
Kynne 153

La Bourdonnais 113
Lafayette 40
Laffey 102
La Galissoniere 113
L'agenais 136
La Prade 150
L'alsacien 136
Lake Champlain 16
Lamons 153
Lancing 153
Lang 145
Lapon 42
Laub 106
La Vallette 104
Lawrence 96
Lawrence C. Taylor 150
Laws 104
Leahy 83
Leander 126
Leary 101
Le Basque 136
Le Bearnais 136
Le Bordelais 136
Le Boulonnais 136
Le Bourguignon 136
Le Brestois 136
Le Breton 136
Le Champenois 136
Le Corse 136
La Gascon 136
Le Formidable 52
Le Foudroyant 52
Le Leland E. Thomas 150
Le Lorrain 136
Leningrad 27
Le Normand 136
Leonard F. Mason 100
Leopard 130
Le Picard 136

Le Provencal 136
Le Ray Wilson 150
Le Redoutable 52
Le Savoyard 136
Leslie L. B. Knox 150
Lester 149
Le Terrible 52
Le Vendeen 136
Levy 153
Lewis and Clark 40
Lexington 16
Leyte 16
Limburg 115
Lincoln 131
Ling 47
Lion 56
Lionfish 47
Little Rock 64
Llandaff 131
Lloyd E. Acree 150
Lloyd Thomas 98
Lockwood 145
Loeser 150
Lofberg 102
London 79
Londonderry 128
Long Beach 57
Los Angeles 62
Lough 150
Lowe 153
Lowestoft 128
Lowry 102
Lübeck 141
Luce 84
Luigi Rizzo 139
Lyman K. Swenson 102
Lynde McCormick 96
Lynx 130

MacDonough 84
Mack 150
MacKenzie 106, 143, 144
Macon 62
Maddox 102
Madison 106
Mahan 84
Maille Breze 113
Major 150
Makigumo 118
Makinami 121
Malcolm 132
Manley 97
Manning 150
Mansfield 102
Maresal Fevzi Cakmak 122
Marchand 153
Margaree 143
Mariano G. Vallejo 40
Marsh 150
Marshall 103
Marsouin 53
Marvin Shields 145
Massey 102
Mayo 106
McCaffery 98
McClelland 153
McCloy 148, 149
McConnell 153
McCook 150
McCord 104
McGinty 150
McKean 101
McKee 104
McLanahan 106
McMorris 149
McNair 103
McNulty 150
Meade 106
Medregal 46
Melbourne 19
Melvin 103
Melvin R. Nawman 150

Menges 153
Menhaden 47
Meredith 100
Merril 153
Mertz 103
Mervine 106
Metcalf 104
Metivier 150
Meyercord 145
Midway 15
Mikhail Kutuzov 66
Miller 104
Mills 153
Minas Gerais 24
Minegumo 118
Minerva 126
Mitscher 85
Moale 102
Mochizvki 118
Mogami 142
Mohawk 129
Moore 153
Morse 53
Morton 97
Moskva 27
Mosley 153
Mullany 104
Mullinix 97
Murasame 120, 121
Murmansk 66
Murphy 106
Murray 132
Myles C. Fox 101
Mysore 77

N *class* 48
Naiad 126
Narval 53
Narwhal 37, 42
Nathanael Greene 40
Nathan Hale 40
Nautilus 44
Neal A. Scott 153
Neunzer 153
New 99
Newell 153
Newman K. Perry 101
New Orleans 26
Newport News 58
Nields 106
Niblack 106
Nicholas 105
Nipigon 143
Noa 100
Noord Brabant 115
Nordkaparen 54
Norfolk 79, 86
Norman Scott 103
Norris 98
Northampton 30
Nubian 129
Nueva Esparta 124
Nueve De Julio 75

O'bannon 105
Oberon 37
Obin 37
O'brien 102
O'callahan 146
Ocelot 37
Ochayanni 112
Odax 46
O'flaherty 150
O'hare 101
Ohi 142
O'higgins 75
Okinawa 26
Oklahoma City 64
Oktyabrskaya Revolutsiya 66
Oliver Mitchell 150
Olympus 37

Onami 121
Onslaught 37
Onyx 37
Opossum 37
Opportune 37
Oracle 37
Ordronaux 106
Oregon City 60
O'reilly 153
Orleck 37
Orpheus 37
Osberg 150
Osiris 37
Osmus 150
Östergötland 116
Osterhaus 153
Oswald 153
Ottawa 143
Otter 37, 150
Otterstetter 153
Otus 37
Otvetsvenni 112
Overijssel 115
Owen 104
Ozbourn 100
Ozhestochonni 112
Ozhivlyonny 112

Palliser 132
Pampanito 47
Parche 47
Pargo 42
Parker 106
Parks 153
Parle 150
Parsons 97
Pasadena 65
Patrick Henry 41
Patterson 145
Paul G. Baker 150
Paul Hamilton 104
Pellew 132
Penelope 126
Perch 47
Perkins 101
Permit 42
Perry 100
Petersen 153, 154
Pettit 153
Philip 105
Philippine Sea 16
Phoebe 126, 127
Picada 47
Pickerel 46
Picking 103
Pintado 42
Piper 47
Pittsburgh 62
Piyale Paşa 122
Plunger 42
Plymouth 128
Pogy 42
Pollack 42
Pomfret 47
Pomodon 46
Poole 153
Pope 153
Porpoise 37
Porqual 37
Porter 103
Porterfield 103
Portsmouth 65
Power 100
Prat 75
Pratt 150
Preble 84
Presley 150
Preston 103
Price 153
Pride 153
Princeton 16
Pritchett 104

158